My Name was Mickey Mantle

Gary Kaschak

Foreword by Bruce Markusen &

New York Times bestselling author Peter Golenbock

Black Rose Writing | Texas

© 2018 by Gary Kaschak
All rights reserved. No part of this book may be reproduced, stored in a retrieval system or transmitted in any form or by any means without the prior written permission of the publishers, except by a reviewer who may quote brief passages in a review to be printed in a newspaper, magazine or journal.

The final approval for this literary material is granted by the author.

First printing

The author has tried to recreate events, locales and conversations from his/her memories. In order to maintain anonymity in some instances, the author may have changed the names of individuals and places. The author may have changed some identifying characteristics and details such as physical properties, occupations and places of residence.

ISBN: 978-1-68433-026-3
PUBLISHED BY BLACK ROSE WRITING
www.blackrosewriting.com

Printed in the United States of America
Suggested Retail Price (SRP) $17.95

My Name was Mickey Mantle is printed in Minion Pro

Dedication

This book is dedicated to my father for teaching me the game of baseball and all its intricacies. Thank you dad, for teaching me the *language* of baseball, for baseball is just that—a language fully comprised of structure and rules that takes time to learn and understand fully. Thanks for throwing me (and to my brothers) a million pitches and hitting a million more. And thanks dad, for showing me through baseball what it takes to be fair.

Thanks, mom, for being at every game and for washing our all-star uniforms in White Birch Lake. Thanks for throwing a thousand dinners together at all hours of the night. And thanks for keeping safety pins in your purse (see chapter 11).

To John and Doug, my brothers. An eternal love of baseball enabled us to create and improvise more games than could possibly be played by two or three people—but we did it. Thanks for the memories.

To Kara and Emily—my best creations (I had some help). Loving and caring nature exemplify such outstanding character and charm in both of you. Thank you for the many softball thrills you provided and for keeping the game alive inside of us during those years.

To my wife, Maureen—the most selfless person there is. Resiliency, tenacity, confidence and humility have shaped you into someone far greater than just a one-of-a-kind. You are the glue—and have been—to *everything*. Oh, and you were a pretty good softball pitcher, too.

Finally, this book is dedicated to the old neighborhood and especially those who'd lived on College Street.

To the Paye's, Cannon's, Mack's, Castelli's, and Barrett's…Thanks for the memories.

Reviews / Blurbs

"*My Name was Mickey Mantle* is not just for Mickey Mantle fans. It's about passion and holding onto childhood…a great read for all ages." –Tom Molito, author of *Mickey Mantle: Inside and Outside The Lines*

"Several dozen Mickey Mantle books are in our research library. None like, My Name was Mickey Mantle—our favorite by far! Great stories not found in any other Commerce Comet book. Get it today!" –Sean Holtz, founder and publisher of *The Baseball Almanac*

"Gary Kaschak's story is about more than the game of baseball. This is a story about his memories, and ours, as baseball fans, and how we look back on the heroes of our youth. We're proud to say his column in the Cooperstown Crier helped lead to this wonderful baseball memoir." –Greg Klein, sports editor, *The Cooperstown Crier*

"In his book, *My Name was Mickey Mantle*, Kaschak sensitively recounts his amazing, (lifetime) imaginative relationship with the legend known only as The Mick." –Allen Meyer, playwright, co-author, *The Signal Season of Dummy Hoy*

"Gary Kaschak's *My Name was Mickey Mantle* gives us a book that is part autobiography, part reminiscence, part hagiography, and part coming-of-age story. Growing up in Binghamton, NY in the 1960s, Kaschak discovered Mantle as an eight-year-old and created a world in which he was Mickey Mantle. He didn't copy Mantle or attempt to be like Mantle—he was Mantle." –Bob Bailey, author of *The History of the Junior World Series*

"Like Gary, from Mickey Mantle I learned to be tough. No Yankee played more games than Mickey while in so much pain. I learned to be patient. Mickey Mantle deeply deserved all the love and all the cheering and all the reverence that he was accorded. Gary's wonderful book certainly proves that." –Peter Golenbock, author of *Idiot* (with Johnny Damon), *Balls* (with Graig Nettles), and *The Bronx Zoo* (with Sparky Lyle)

Acknowledgements

To Bruce Markusen and Peter Golenbock for setting the tone for the story with outstanding Forewords. I am grateful beyond words.

To Tommy Molito, author of *Mickey Mantle Inside and Outside* the *Lines*, for taking a fair amount of time with me talking about Mickey Mantle and the old Yankees, and especially for reading my manuscript and supporting its potential.

To Margaret Hadsell, Town of Vestal Historian, for researching archived newspapers and for allowing me (and my mother) access to them. Your diligent research firmed up a few loose ends.

To Ron Ohnmacht, (former Vestal Little League Board Member) for establishing the original website for the Vestal Little League, and for providing my Vestal Police Little League team photo from 1968.

To Vestal Little League President Stace Kintner for arranging a tour of Angelo Field, my old Little League ballpark.

To my old Little League teammate, Dr. Mark Mysnyk and to his mother Laura Mysynk for efforts in locating old Little League photos from 1968.

To Nick Marco. Coach, thanks for making me a better writer.

To Gordon Allen, editor of the old Vestal News. Thanks for hiring me as sports-writer and laying the foundation.

To Sonny Pomponio for generously *giving me* his one copy of an August 18th, 1961 *Life* magazine featuring Mickey Mantle and Roger Maris on its cover. Very cool.

To Reagan Rothe (Publisher of Black Rose Writing). Thanks a million for taking a chance on me.

My Name was Mickey Mantle

Foreword by Bruce Markusen

I have no recollection of seeing Mickey Mantle play, none whatsoever. But that doesn't mean that I didn't see him play. I have it on good authority that I did watch him play; that is what several of my family members have told me. It was 1968, when I was all of three years old and Mantle was playing what turned out to be his final major league season for the New York Yankees. My family has often told me that I would plant myself in front of our black-and-white television in Bronxville, NY, and watch Yankee games at that age—too young for me to remember, of course. They say that my excitement level grew whenever Mantle stepped into the batter's box. That's when I would begin to jump up and down hysterically, with my sudden movements accompanied by a few discernible yells. The loud noises would continue throughout the at-bat, only to be resurrected the next time that Mantle stepped into the batter's box.

I don't remember any of this, but when three different family members—my father, my sister and my godmother—tell you that it happened, it must have. Perhaps it's further proof of the impact that Mantle had on baseball fans in the New York metropolitan area, powerful enough to persuade a young three-year-old boy to pay such attention, at a time when attention spans are not exactly at their lengthiest. Even the mere mention of the name Mickey Mantle cast a spell over a young child, one who was too young to discern much of what was going on in day-to-day life. Mickey Mantle had that power, the power to overcome such obstacles, the power to penetrate a three-year-old mind and captivate it.

I can only imagine that my father, Stan, who was a diehard baseball fan, must have told me about Mantle and the importance that he held in baseball at the time. My father was a fan of the expansion New York Mets, but he understood that I had somehow adopted the Yankees as my team. He must have filled my ears with stories of the Yankees, their legendary history, and the exploits of the player who had become the franchise's most popular performer of the 1950s and sixties.

As I grew older in the early 1970s, I became a diehard fan and follower of the Yankees, but lost my interest in Mantle, who become somewhat of a forgotten figure to me. As with most younger fans, I had little interest in past history; I was far more consumed with the Yankees of the here and now, the Yankees of Thurman Munson and Bobby Murcer, my current day heroes. I remember when the Alou brothers (Felipe and Matty) played for the team, along with a young Jewish designated hitter named Ron Blomberg. I remember the colorful figures, like Fritz Peterson and Sparky Lyle. I remember some of the past-their-prime veterans who passed through the clubhouse, players like Johnny Callison and Jim Ray Hart and Ron Swoboda and Sam McDowell. They were brand-name players, players who had long since enjoyed their best days, but they were still the Yankees of my youth.

Quite frankly, it was not until the mid-1990s that I started to think about Mickey Mantle again. This occurred, not so coincidently, at the same time that I left my job working as a sports talk show host in Utica, NY, giving up that career path to take a position working in the library of the National Baseball Hall of Fame and Museum. By the 1990s, I had started to become consumed with baseball history, particularly with baseball from the 1960s and seventies. I suppose that's why I left sports talk radio to concentrate on a baseball research position, allowing me to fully immerse myself within the game's history, learn more about, and begin writing about it.

I joined the staff of the Hall of Fame in March of 1995. That was right about the time that Mickey Mantle's deteriorating health began to make national headlines. For years, Mantle had abused alcohol—that was no secret, any baseball fan knew about Mantle's reputation for drinking and hard living—but now the situation had reached rather dire circumstances. Diagnosed with both cirrhosis and hepatitis, Mantle needed a liver transplant—badly. Without it, he would die.

As his health declined, Mantle only grew in stature with me. For several years, he had talked willingly about his failures—and he was only more willing to do so now. Convinced that he was going to die young, he had abused his body through alcohol and late nights, something that he now regretted. He acknowledged having been a failure as both a husband and a father. He admitted that he had failed as a role model, letting down fans and teammates along the way. In his own down-home way, he told kids not to repeat the mistakes that he had made, but rather to learn from them and choose a better path. That willingness to admit mistakes, and to do so in front of millions, told us something about this man.

A few months after hearing reports that Mantle needed a liver transplant, he received one. But as doctors prepared to replace his liver, they realized that his liver was cancerous, and that the cancer had spread. The doctors completed the transplant, but realized that it would have no long-term impact. Not long after, Mantle died, leaving us all too soon at the age of 63. In the months leading up to his death, there was speculation that Mantle was readying himself for a return to Cooperstown for the annual Induction Ceremonies. Finding himself overwhelmed by the rush of fans during his first visit to Cooperstown, he had not returned for an induction since the early 1970s. But by the 1990s, his Hall of Fame friends had begun to convince him that the situation was different now, that with additional security in Cooperstown, he would not feel so overcome by the crowds and could truly enjoy the weekend experience.

Sadly, Mantle never had that chance, the cancer taking him away just as he seemed ready to return to Cooperstown. As a result, I never had the opportunity to meet my boyhood idol. I had met numerous Hall of Famers over the years, but Mantle had always eluded my grasp.

In retrospect, I feel alright with that. After all, Mantle had the kind of down-to-earth personality that came across so beautifully in interviews and public appearance. Even listening to Mantle speak from afar, I felt like I knew him—at least a little bit. I felt like I could sit down and have a cup of coffee with him, while carrying on a conversation with someone so approachable and charming. And then, upon hearing the stories of other Yankee players, who so often talked about Mantle being the best of teammates, I felt even better about my relationship with a man I had never met.

Even though I never talked to him, and really don't remember seeing Mantle play, his impact on my life became profound. As much as any individual player, he is the reason that I became a fan of this game, the man who piqued by baseball interest at the tender age of three. And when my love of baseball became stronger through my growing appreciation of its history, Mantle only strengthened those feelings.

For all of that, I owe Mickey Mantle a lot. Thank you, Mick.

Bruce Markusen has worked at the National Baseball Hall of Fame as manager of digital and outreach learning, manager of program presentations, and as a senior researcher. He has written seven books on baseball, including *A Baseball Dynasty: Charlie Finley's Swingin' A's*, the winner of the Seymour Medal.

He resides in Cooperstown with his wife, Sue, and his daughter, Maddie.

Foreword by Peter Golenbock

I have always contended that baseball is the one religion that unifies us rather than divides us. There is a common bond among true baseball fans that brings strangers together as family. You can be white, black, brown, Jewish, gay or an American Indian, if you love baseball and the other person loves baseball, you are connected as a very special way. In the abstract, Yankee fans hate Red Sox fans and vice versa, but if you the Yankee fan ever sat down next to a Red Sox fan and began to discuss the game in any serious way, you discover that deep down both of you love the game so much that when you're talkin' baseball, you're able to put aside your differences and revel in the common bond.

I teach a class on the history of baseball at the University of South Florida, St. Petersburg campus. I talk about the songs that bind the sport: *Take Me Out to the Ballgame*, of course, but such standards as *Have You Seen Jackie Robinson Hit That Ball, Centerfield, Willie, Mickey, and the Duke*, and *I Love Mickey* by Theresa Brewer. There is the scripture of the game, books like *Glory of Their Times, Ball Four,* and *The Boys of Summer.*

Baseball, unlike traditional religions, doesn't have one God. Rather, baseball gives you a panorama of Gods that you may pick and choose from. They change with each generation. Before the turn of the century there was the heroic Michael King Kelly. The song *Slide, Kelly, Slide,* was written for him. His pictures appeared on more gin joint walls than any other American. The lithograph of King Kelly sliding into home plate replaced the lithograph of Custer's Last Stand in most of those bars in the 1880s.

For rooters of a certain age there was Joe Jackson and Tyrus Raymond Cobb, the two greatest hitters who ever lived. Jackson was beloved, even though he was wrongly thrown out of baseball after being part of the Black Sox conspiracy of 1919, and Cobb was beloved, even though he was a nasty bigot, because he had a lifetime batting average of .367. Christy Mathewson was beloved for being a Christian gentleman while winning 373 games for The New York Giants. He was gassed while in the Army and died at a young age, earning him the designation of Saint Christy. The other saint in the baseball heavens is Lou Gehrig, who toiled in Babe Ruth's giant shadow until he suffered the incurable disease that was named after him. When he was honored by the Yankees just before his death, he proclaimed that he was "the luckiest man on the face of the earth." Swiftly sainthood followed.

Ruth, of course, was the most popular baseball player in the history of the sport. Ruth made everyone forget about the Black Sox scandal, and he led the Red Sox and the Yankees into an amazing ten World Series. Ruth hit 714 home runs and drove in 2211 runs. He was The Bambino and The Sultan of Swat.

It's not written about, but in the history of the game there was one other player whose popularity equaled The Babe's. For the boys and girls of my – and Gary's —generation, the post-World War II baby boomers, a blond youngster named Mickey Mantle emigrated to the Bronx from the far-off frontier state of Oklahoma in 1951 with straw between his teeth and thunder in his bat.

But that wasn't all. He could fly from home plate to first base faster than any other player in the game, and in the outfield he could chase down balls that seemed impossible to catch. Plus he had a rifle for an arm. He would throw out runners at home plate from his station in center field, leaving us incredulous and giddy.

More often than not we learned of his exploits from a prophet by the name of Mel Allen, who brought the message from God to us through a hand-sized rectangle with the fancy name of Magnavox on its case. It was a radio powered by tiny mysterious transistors that managed to bring Allen's mellifluous voice and the roar of the crowd all the way from his microphone to my transistor radio that I held next to my ear as I lay in bed at night as I fought off sleep so I could listen to the Yankee games.

I lived in Stamford, Connecticut, a 45-minute hop, step, and a jump by rail to Grand Central Station and then on to the Taj Mahal-like Stadium via the Lexington Avenue number 6 train. The thrill of the trip always came when the subway emerged from the darkness to rise up onto the raised platform as the train pulled into the stop overlooking the Stadium.

Though trips to the Stadium were rare, I was lucky enough to have an RCA TV in my bedroom on the second floor of our suburban home, and since I was the only one living up there (my brother and sister had rooms on the first floor), I could watch the night games (and Johnny Carson) without fear of parental interruption. You talk about Heaven on Earth. This was it.

I loved the Yankees with all my heart. I was an over privileged private school kid, and it bothered me not a whit that the Yankees – with Mickey Mantle leading the way – managed to win the pennant year after year after year.

Okay, we didn't win in 1954 because the Cleveland Indians won 111 games, and we didn't win in 1959 because – to this day I still don't know why we didn't win. Billy Pierce and Luis Aparicio had something to do with it. But until my second year of college during those years of childhood, led by Mickey, Yogi, Whitey, and Roger, since 1951 the Yankees won fourteen pennants in sixteen years – and as far as I was concerned, they did it for me.

If someone had asked me, "Who would you rather be, Superman or Mickey Mantle?" It wasn't close, though I loved Steve Reeves in Superman. I would have proudly proclaimed: Mickey Mantle. (As you will see Gary once chose Batman over Mickey Mantle, and it cost him dearly.)

When I played in the backyard as a kid – just as Gary did —I held my bat the way Mickey held his, with the pinky finger of my left hand *under* the barrel of the bat the way Mickey hit when he batted right-handed. I switch hit the way Mickey did for a short while, hoping my left-handed skills would improve, but I didn't hit enough left-handed and had to give it up. I ran like Mickey Mantle, running with purpose and with pumping knees. I played stick ball batting like Mickey Mantle with Paul Housman and Bobby Nemiroff and once hit a ball out of our yard that broke into a million pieces a second-floor bedroom window of the Housman's home. That moment I could not have been happier.

I owned a Mickey Mantle Rawlings glove, which I oiled periodically so it wouldn't dry out, and sometimes I would sleep with my glove. The fingers on my left hand felt snug in its leathery warmth.

I loved candy, and I ended up being cavity prone, and when I would go to the dentist to have a cavity-infected tooth drilled, I would picture Mickey Mantle standing at the plate as the dentist began to inflict his pain. I'd close my eyes and watch in my mind's eye as Mantle hit a long home run and then slowly circled the bases with that determined stride of his. By the time he reached home plate, my dental ordeal would be over.

I never told anyone about any of this, of course. It was none of anyone else's business. And from what I've come to understand, at least until reading Gary's fine book, other kids didn't share their baseball obsessions either.

Like Gary, from Mickey Mantle I learned to be tough. No Yankee played more games than Mickey while in so much pain. I learned to be patient. I learned what it took to play the game, and like Gary, from Mickey I learned strength of character.

Not for a minute did I think I was doing anything extraordinary in any way. And when Mickey won the MVP trophy in 1956, 1957, and 1961 I didn't think that what he was doing was extraordinary either. I felt that his performing on that level was somehow related to my fervent desire for him to be that great.

I wished. He hit. It was that simple. But it worked both ways. It also gave me the notion in my head that if I tried hard enough, like Mickey I could accomplish anything I set my mind to do. My baseball dreams remained intact until I turned 13.

At that age I was playing in a baseball game after class at St. Luke's School. Or it might have been a gym class. Up to this point I was certain I was going to eventually replace Mickey Mantle as the Yankee centerfielder (This was 1959, and I had no idea he would play until 1968.) I got up right-handed, and the pitcher, Michael Smith, threw me a pitch that was headed straight for my head. I stepped in the bucket as the ball dipped and dived and slammed into the catcher's glove. Strike one. He threw me two more of those pitches, and each time I flinched and took the pitch for a strike. It was at that point that I knew I wouldn't be taking Mickey's spot in centerfield. (It took Gary a few years more to utter the words, 'I wasn't Mickey Mantle, and was beginning to understand I never would be."

I decided if I couldn't play major league baseball, I would write about it. As a freshman I began writing for The Daily Dartmouth newspaper, and I was thrilled to find myself in the presence of athletic director Red Rolfe, who had been the New York Yankees' third baseman in the 1930s and 1940s. His teammates were the legendary Joe DiMaggio and Bill Dickey, and we would sit for hours and talk baseball. Red had graduated from Dartmouth and for a while had coached baseball at Dartmouth after his Yankee career ended.

After three years in law school I ended up using my legal training as a writer for Prentice-Hall. I wrote a weekly column about President Nixon's wage and price controls. After six weeks of this I strolled down the halls to knock on the door of the head editor of Prentice-Hall's trade book division. I had seen some of their books. Lawrence Welk wrote one called "Ah One, Ah Two." Willie Sutton, a famous bank robber, wrote a book called "That's Where The Money Is."

As a kid rummaging through the Stamford Library sports books, I discovered a book called *The New York Yankees* by Frank Graham. It was published in 1948, and it told stories about Babe Ruth, Lou Gehrig, and all the Yankee greats from the founding of the franchise to 1948. I had always held it in the back of my mind that I would write the sequel to Graham's memorable book. I had first called the Yankees' PR department to ask if I could use their files as material if I could get a book contract. I was told I could. I was also told there was no way I would ever get a book contract.

I walked through the door and introduced myself. I told the editor, Nick D'Incecco, about my desire to write about the fourteen pennants that the Yankees had won in sixteen years. I told him the Yankees had given me permission to go through their archive. He had me write a short proposal for the project. I listed the names of the players I would write about. It was a long list of famous Yankee players.

D'Incecco, it turned out, also was a crazy Yankee fan who loved Mickey Mantle, Yogi Berra, and Whitey Ford. He gave me a contract and paid me $2,500 in advance.

I drove to Yankee Stadium to begin my research. It was the fall of 1972, and Mike Burke of CBS, a lovely, urbane man, was in charge of the team. His PR director, Bob Fishel, made me feel welcome, and I was in heaven. When there was no one in the office, it wasn't long before I was answering the phone, "New York Yankees."

I got to go to lunch with the Yankee brass. I got to shag flies for a few of the players. I got to watch as Thurman Munson spit tobacco juice on my shoes. Meanwhile I must have gone through thousands of old newspaper clippings to discover that you can't write a book using newspaper clippings.

I knew what I had to do. I had to go and interview the players of my youth. I had to get in the car, or use the train or plane, to go see them. I went to Nick D'Incecco and told him what I wanted to do.

He gave me another $2,500.

I did research in Cooperstown, so the first player I went to see was former pitcher Jim Konstanty, who lived close to the Hall of Fame. He showed me the movies he had taken when the Yankees went to Japan after the 1956 season. I visited all the players from the New York metropolitan area, Phil Rizzuto, Eddie Lopat, Joe Pepitone, Yogi Berra, Joe Collins, Ellie Howard, Gil McDougald, and Phil Linz. Whitey Ford, who lived on Long Island, came and visited me in the Roger Williams Hotel where I was living in New York City.

I got on a plane and flew to California to interview Don Larsen, Andy Carey, Johnny Lindell, and owner Del Webb. I caught up with Allie Reynolds, Norm Siebern, Tom Sturdivant, Jerry Lumpe, Johnny Kucks, Bob Cerv, and Hank Bauer in the states of Oklahoma, Missouri, and Kansas. I spent a day in Commerce, Oklahoma, to see first-hand just how poor Mickey Mantle was growing up.

I was out of money, and Nick D'Incecco gave me another $2,500.

The player I wished to interview most of all was Mickey, and we arranged for me to visit him at his home in Dallas. When I arrived at the Dallas airport, I called his house and was told that he had just gotten on a plane to go to New

York for Old-Timers' Day.

The next morning I caught the earliest plane to New York, and when I arrived at the Stadium, I went into the Yankee clubhouse. There was Mickey, dressed in his finest cowboy browns. I'm not usually shy, but I just couldn't bring myself to approach him. I asked Ellie Howard, a lovely man, if he would do it for me, and he was only too happy to oblige.

"Mick, may I ask you a few questions?" I said.

He looked at me and with a grin he said, "No." And very quickly, "Sure."

He must have seen the crestfallen look on my face, because he laughed. And then he gave me one of the finest, most personal interviews I ever conducted. He had retired in 1968, and this was 1973, and he began to tell me how much he missed playing, that the only reason he quit was that he no longer was healthy enough to play the game. He talked about his nightmares, how he would be sleeping, and in his dream he could hear Bob Shepard, the PA announcer, say, "Now batting, number 7, Mickey Mantle," and Mickey said he would find himself outside the stadium unable to find the door to get in.

"I'd wake up in a sweat," he said.

When he was telling me about how he had injured himself by stepping into a sprinkler head in right field, wrecking his knee, he told me that when he got out of the cab to the hospital, his father had gone with him. He said that he leaned on his father's shoulder – at this point he put his arms on my right shoulder and pushed down, and I could feel the raw power in his arms. He said when he leaned on his father like that, his father collapsed to the ground. Mickey didn't know it at the time, but his father had cancer and was dying. They went into the hospital together. His father would die not long afterwards.

What I noticed most about Mantle was his modesty.

"I struck out 1,500 times and walked 1,500 times," he said. "That's five years' worth of doing nothing."

Mickey made it clear that he wasn't much interested in fame and what that fame had brought him.

I was able to tell him how much he meant to me, and to all the other Yankee fans.

"I wish I had realized that when I was playing," he said. "I'd have been nicer to all those people."

That book, *Dynasty: The New York Yankees 1949-1964*, was published in 1975. It is still in print today, more than 40 years later, by Dover Press. In it, Mickey comes alive again.

Since writing that first book, I was privileged to be able to write books with other Yankees, specifically Billy Martin, Ron Guidry, and Graig Nettles. I wrote *Wild, High & Tight,* Billy Martin's biography, and I also wrote *7, the Mickey Mantle Novel.*

Over the years because of my friendship with Billy Martin, I got to spend quality time with him and Mickey, who I discovered to be one of the funniest people I ever knew. His jokes put me on the floor. His off-color jokes in *7* will put you on the floor. Mickey was also one of the most humble people I ever knew. That was the point of *7*, to show how funny and how humble Mickey was. It was a controversial book, the same way *Ball Four* by Jim Bouton was controversial, because some rigid people don't always want to hear the truth. They'd rather be spoon-fed the legend.

One thing I do know: Mickey Mantle deeply deserved all the love and all the cheering and all the reverence that he was accorded. Gary's wonderful book certainly proves that. Mickey Mantle not only was a great baseball player, he was a great role model - —regardless of his excesses —for me, for Gary, and for literally millions of other boys and girls of our generation.

Gods, it turns out, don't have an easy time being Gods.

Preface

I've never written a memoir or a coming- of-age story. In fact, I hadn't seriously considered it. I emphasize *never*, since the thought had occurred that one day I'd write mine— likely in old age with nothing better to do. Then something deeply profound happened to help change that timeline.

Dreams. Many dreams. Dreams spread over 20 incredible days that spun like a mini-series of my young life, running in perfect sequence to my age. They centered squarely on my baseball playing years, beginning with age eight, nine, then 10 and beyond. They pulled me so far inside that it felt as if I was part of them, that I was *really there* playing baseball all day long and into the night. Dreams turned to notes and notes turned to chapters. A book was born.

Admitting to myself that a coming-of-age story wouldn't be interesting enough to anyone outside of family was a tough obstacle to overcome. But what happened during this magical trip down memory lane has given me a new resolve and has changed my mind. Now, it is with steadfast conviction and belief that my story is representative to millions of baseball stories that have gone untold from ordinary people like me. But that is the beauty of it all, really. For it is this strength in numbers and millions of experiences and stories that fortifies the commonality we share.

Most of us have been in the backyard, the street or sandlot playing baseball when we'd step to the plate in the bottom of the 9th in game seven of the World Series, bases loaded, two outs and trailing by three runs. Fouling off pitch after pitch to keep faint hopes alive, we knew the next pitch was the one that would change everything. And with providence stepping in to lend a hand, it did. With a mighty swing of the bat producing a sound like none before, the next baseball legend was born. And as that ball rose and landed into uncharted distances of any home run ever before, we took the bases and seized the day—Roy Hobbs style.

As I've looked back when childhood heroes were made, something peculiar is worth mentioning. Not once had I imagined *myself* being that World Series hero. Never had I imagined *Gary Kaschak* as the one hitting a game-winning home run to win the World Series for my New York Yankees. Instead, I could be only *Mickey Mantle* when it came to baseball. It's just the way it was.

While the deeper inside story illustrates my unique and unusual relationship with Mickey Mantle, I stress this now to aid in its believability. Although I was introduced to Mickey Mantle when I was about seven or eight years old, I'd never met him. I never shook his hand or came any closer to him than from a seat on the mezzanine section of Yankee Stadium. What we had instead was a deeply personal *relationship*—and one I'd never mentioned to another soul until now.

It mattered *some* when I'd discovered more about Mickey Mantle and his lifestyle off the field, but it wasn't enough to abandon him. Mickey had never abandoned me when I'd called upon him at every integral part of my baseball. I carried Mickey on my shoulder at every game as if he had been a shadow. I believed he was guiding me in making the right decisions, and together we were invincible.

But as time moved on, I wasn't able always to make Mickey proud of me. I failed sometimes. Not in striking out or in making the last out of a game, but in making important decisions involving character and integrity. And while such decisions pale to Mickey Mantle's decisions and admissions, I had no right judging him and wouldn't be one to cast the first stone.

I hope you enjoy the journey I've taken with Mickey Mantle. I hope you can identify with its chapter by chapter process, for that is what it has been to me. I hope you can feel and understand any emotions I'd felt, the evolution of the story and in its truly remarkable, spiritual ending. My further hope is that my personal stories serve to trigger and free your memories of playing baseball all day long and into the night, and help you remember how great it all really was.

Gary Kaschak

1

Beginnings

Just about every kid who played baseball at some point in life had a favorite player. Mine was Mickey Mantle.

Uniquely personal my admiration and devotion was to Mickey, but not exclusive by any means. Millions of kids from east to west and all points in between professed an unusual love and approbation for the greatest player of them all—no different than mine. And while the number of Mantle copycats seemed to grow exponentially by the day, none could match Mickey's batting stance or run the bases with the same hitch and limp as I could. And they couldn't hit or field their positions like Mickey, either.

Yet, they kept on trying.

I knew deep down all the way to my soul how fraudulent these claims were. And although I was just nine years old, this nonsense was beginning to get to me. I had wondered long and often why it had been so hard for others to recognize the signs of baseball greatness that had been passed down to me, of how the honor to call oneself Mickey Mantle had been meant for me and me alone. There could be no sharing his name with any other boy for much longer. Something needed to be done to bring out the truth in the matter.

Proving and defending such a claim came with certain grounds rules, for this was territory unlike all others. Mickey Mantle's name was synonymous with baseball perfection, and the grounds rules of local baseball was needed to prove to those standing in the, *wanna be* Mickey line, to just, *forget about it*. The tipping-point had reached its end—it was time for the whole truth to be revealed to a sea of imposters falling short in emulating Mickey Mantle. Although challengers would be defeated in just my neighborhood, it didn't matter that much, for that insulated bubble on the map I called home was the most important territory to conquer. Neighborhoods in any direction from home were mostly unknown, as were identities, personalities and baseball talents of many kids who'd lived there. Certainly within those borders and beyond, hundreds more wanted to be Mickey Mantle—probably thousands. And while I planned to one day take my game further into uncharted waters of Binghamton's west side and beyond, concerns at protecting a narrow territory of a four-block radius called the fourth ward was more pragmatic. Taking the matter outside my isolated four-block world was enticing, but out of the question for now—and with good reason. Certain areas we wouldn't breach—usually. Every so often we'd get up some courage to cross invisible lines of neighborhoods, or at least to venture out along the rim of so called borders. We understood an unwritten rule held us back from penetrating certain points, and staying safe and unharmed from bullies seemed the most prudent choice of all. Despite such invisible barriers, I was certain challengers from outside would be defeated easily. Harnessed as I was from exploring the deeper reaches of the city, conquering an area as narrow as my neighborhood would have to do for now and likely would be temporary. Unable to pursue and vanquish other bordering neighborhoods as the King of Baseball would take some time.

Sure, I'd analyze and judge competitors, understanding stances others had taken. Contemplating what all of us wanted was understandable, for who could blame any boy or girl for trying out for the part of Mickey Mantle? Taking it all in stride and reminding myself of *who I was*, and how I'd need to prove myself seemed to work best at maintaining focus. Words and bravado from thousands of frauds could never equate to the true-life version of Mickey Mantle that only I seemed capable of duplicating.

Proof in the matter would be earned and won honorably on the fields of Binghamton's Recreation Park, or the nearby playgrounds of Horace Mann School. Of course it would have to be the field of play where talent and results would give up the truth, for the diamond couldn't lie. Power and speed and clutch hitting could not go unnoticed, could not go unrewarded. Combined baseball elements that so defined me could no longer be kept secret, and harboring this gospel truth with a saintly patience had been bottled up long enough. My time had arrived. Refined baseball talents like no other boy ready to bust loose on the field of play. Pure and simple it seemed to me, just like the game itself seemed. Proving myself to cynics was vitally necessary. And when that time arrived finally and the dust from the base paths cleared, there was no doubting what I had known all along, for God-given talents and preparation had a way in revealing itself. Performance under such conditions erased any misgivings others may have had. The local proving grounds had indeed given up the truth. And at the end of the day one thing was certain; I was the one *and only one* with the pedigree to lift that sword from its stone. *My name was Mickey Mantle.*

Such childhood memories of days spent as Mickey Mantle began surfacing a few years ago, at first just a few thoughts, then the dreams. One by one they'd line up in my sleep, a 20-day cycle as clear and vivid and as real as though I'd actually been there. The smells and sounds of baseball and everything else surrounded me in absolute detail. And as old baseball memories poured out in perfect sequence to age, pinpointing specific reasons as to why such sudden and dramatic visions appeared are pure guesses. But I have a hunch it stems from a lengthy baseball project involving a player from the 19th century I'd been researching. Innocuous as it seems, that project is likely the culprit to all this madness. Perhaps all the baseball research had opened up a portal creating an avalanche of baseball stories seeping from the corners of my mind. As a few days passed and visions and dreams continued, I'd felt compelled to begin writing it all down. Logging and maintaining a record seemed the logical thing to do. And so I did.

In a few nights, I became captivated and hoped and prayed that the dreams continued. I wanted to stay inside them and to wake up as that nine-year old boy. The dreams seemed better than any hallucinate or drug, and certainly as addicting as one—no wonder that was. Escaping into my past and playing baseball all day long released me from my troubles. Deep-seated memories somehow merged in this crazy way, allowing me to manage, control and even induce them just before bedtime. Profound and in perfect sequence they spun. Age 8, then 9 then 10 and beyond, blending perfectly like chapters to a book.

But as the dreams continued, a bit more clouded and hazy they became.

Perhaps the fantasy life led as a boy was running parallel to age, that growing older eroded childhood thoughts as well as the ability to see things as they were. Abandoning childish behavior ever so gradually gave way to things more worldly, and by the time I'd reached age 12, the clear visions had nearly vanished.

As these magnificent memories and dreams reached an end, I'd felt compelled, nudged into taking notes I'd made and to write this book. I supposed that such thoughts and memories had a deeper purpose, somehow more than just a wonderful trip for one down memory lane. Much more seemed to be going on. Contemplating and absorbing such terribly egotistical thoughts helped me come to my senses—at least for a while. But negative thoughts ran in tandem, running their Devil's advocate course of interference and doing their devil's best to wake me from this pretense of thinking so highly of myself and of my story. Personal significance of commonplace memories and how trite mine might seem blocked the big picture from coming into full view—at least for a while. Thoughts of watching home videos or being shown pictures of newborn babies from total strangers came to mind. Little impact most likely they'd have on me, and likely little to others. As much as I tried deflecting such personal thoughts of self-centeredness, they remained at the forefront. My mind continued experiencing similar thoughts about this book, but it seemed only natural. My viewpoint certainly excited me, but what about others? What would reactions be? Why in the world would anyone outside of friends and family show an interest in this story? What would compel anyone to read the book, cover to cover, and to buy into its premise? As question after question raced through my mind, I took the next step and began asking adults around my age to recount and share personal baseball tales from the past. Perhaps I'd find some answers here.

While this unscientific survey didn't cross borders beyond my perch in South Jersey, I spoke with dozens of folks from far and wide. As I made notes to fascinating and riveting stories, I'd discovered something somewhat surprising, yet not surprising at all. For even those born and raised outside of Yankee territory professed an unusual draw to Mickey Mantle. Certainly they'd rooted for other teams and players in closer geographic proximity to home, but it was Mickey Mantle ruling the roost of popularity, hands down.

When asked about a favorite player, Mickey Mantle's name was the first spoken nearly unanimously.

As these engaging interviews continued, my newfound baseball friends opened up willingly, jumping at the chance to talk baseball past. I felt a natural connection, as if I'd been talking to best friends at some baseball reunion. Stories flowed freely about Mickey Mantle, other players and teams, told in remarkable detail as if they'd happened yesterday—no different than my experiences. Thorough and seamless they came, fabulous stories told from the heart. Common threads to stories ran parallel to mine. Tales and yarns unalterable, only names and places were different. We struck a very special bond through baseball.

I started warming up to the idea not to be afraid to tell the story. Perhaps my personal trove of Mickey Mantle stories was worthy enough to share with others, and that baseball-lovers would enjoy it. As the strength and unusual energy generated from memories filtered through me, I'd taken note to a huge advantage from the dreams. Able I was to take an introspective look inside myself *as that boy*, with ability to decipher replaying stories through the eyes of my adult self. I could watch myself grow and mature from that young boy, observing stories unfolding from my adult position. Inevitable outcomes aside, this dynamic revelation gave me the feeling of being sent back in time, almost as if I'd been spying on myself—empowering and rich the feeling, almost beyond comprehension.

And as these fingerprints, blueprints and photographs from the mind revealed themselves in far greater detail than any dream before, much more seemed to be at stake beyond just baseball. The dreams extended beyond playing baseball or believing I was Mickey Mantle, for a veritable potpourri of what once was came into view, showing me vast experiences during times of innocence, chock-full of fond memories from the culture and what the promise of youth held for us. Snapshots and albums loaded and locked into the minds-eye, streaming videos playing out in entire episodes. And as I watched and remembered and longed for those days, I thought about the promise of youth and what it meant to many of us back then. As these virtual episodes spun freely in my minds eye, nostalgic thoughts prevailed. As the naivety of being that boy in the 60's gripped me like a vice, I remembered that simple life. I remembered how good it seemed and how easy life was. All of it came into view and flooded my being.

For those baby-boomers and older folks reading this now, you'll likely understand and remember. For any younger readers, well, some lessons in history are always good to learn. Although I may be taking a long trip down memory lane here, I find it to be vital to the story, to what I'd experienced in the dreams, and how the innocent times of the early and mid-1960's have impacted this story. Please indulge me.

There were no cell-phones, Internet or video games to play, no malls to hang out in and very little loafing around the house or expressing boredom for long. For what we had instead was engrained within ourselves. It lived in our imaginations and the freedom of the great outdoors. And while those simple choices seem so distant and (sadly) virtually obsolete by today's standards, they were perfect for the times. Perhaps those few years in the 60's were the very last years of the age of innocence, or perhaps those wonder years bordered along the fringes of innocence—at least as we knew it. A crossroad giving way to developing technology that would soon enough alter the landscape of youth and innocence as we had experienced. And as cultures shift and change for every generation, growing up in the 60's was a time of innocence and for good reason.

Telephones were ruled by the "party line," an intricate system of shared lines. Phone conversation between adults was usually infrequent with minimal chatting. The ability for a third party to interrupt any call was routine, and while eavesdropping was possible, I believe that is was rare, for manners and honor prevailing within the culture was expected at most times. Mutual respect is what was shared by the majority. But due to the odd arrangement, children rarely used the telephone, or for that matter even wanted to. There was no need to talk to a friend you'd been playing with all day, and on rare times when we wanted to contact someone by phone, time restrictions of usually five minutes were applied. And we listened and obeyed those orders. Not six or seven minutes. Five minutes and done.

Television had similar limitations. Three channels, no remote control, black and white sets for families lucky enough to afford one. And yes, just one set per household. Fuzzy and grainy the images appeared on the screen, with scattered signals that flickered and wavered, forcing us to alter the "rabbit ears" antenna at multiple angles until a better signal returned. And while the

TV was there for us, most of us kids watched just a few shows per week, the Saturday morning cartoon extravaganza that played on through the early afternoon hours our favorite day of all.

The world outside was in flux. Communist Russia was our enemy and we knew it. We'd learned of their desire for global domination, scaring us out of our wits. Told and warned we learned of their desire to launch missiles halfway across the world at us, with little understanding as to why our small-town Binghamton would be a potential target for an incoming bomb. "Communism" just seemed like a big word for "hate," and spreading hate across the world seemed to be their intent. It's what we knew and grew up with.

A government sponsored readiness plan was established and sent for us to learn and practice in school, preparing us from any pending atomic bomb strike launched by the "Iron Curtain" of Russia. "Duck and Cover" was its name. Cute and clever in delivering such persuasion, with animated ducks pictured on a pamphlet, they introduced us to the world of war with detailed instructions, pictures and diagrams of what to do to survive. They illustrated how to remain calm, how not to panic during and after a bombardment by the enemy. As archaic as it sounds today, it was serious business in its day. We practiced the exercises as often as routine fire drills that kept us on our toes. We burrowed underneath our little desks like rodents looking for cover against marauding predators. And while we may have protected ourselves against the potential of shattering glass and debris strewn across the room from the blast zone, there was no talk of nuclear fallout and its ramifications. Never had we heard of what could happen had we been lucky enough to survive the impact of a bomb. Fallout and all its consequences had never been mentioned to us even once—at least to my memory.

Images of war cluttered our impressionable minds from the few war movies we'd watched, even the war comic books we'd read. Gory images prevailed—nightmare images. After all, bombs killed people, and hiding underneath a desk was little or no protection against one. Despite it all, we practiced our routines. We prepared for the day. We believed what we'd been told with an innocence and trust in the system.

Milk was delivered to homes in glass bottles. Whole milk, cold and fresh. Giddy attendants greeted us at the local filling station, an army of men dressed in neatly pressed white uniforms. Feverishly they set about their tasks, in tandem checking the oil, pumping the gas and cleaning the windows. Overboard they went with their service. Insanely polite they were. Oh, and a full tank of gas was rewarded, a set of drinking glasses the usual gift—the Flintstones cartoon characters my personal favorite of all.

And we bought into everything because there was no choice. Everything we'd learned came strictly from the adults in charge of us. And what was told by the government was the gospel truth—especially true if such words had been spoken from the president himself. And if something had been taught to us by anyone in charge, well, that too was gospel. No challenging of its merit, no room for debate. We believed *everything* we'd been taught.

Reference books were full of just enough basic facts they wanted us to know. History books undoubtedly followed a consistent path of rhetoric for decades, but we didn't know any better. History books or encyclopedias containing information that didn't seem right, well, there was no challenging that. For if it had been written, it must be so.

Naïve and innocent we were. The school and public library was the only means to learn more about the world. Occasional visits to the library restricted us to age-appropriate books. As this carefree age of innocence played on before us, we played on with an assortment of toys and games that ruled the day. Simple toys and games consisting of basic challenges to stir the mind like Lincoln Logs, Etch-a-sketch or a Kaleidoscope. Many of us owned a slinky or a pogo stick. Monopoly and checkers were our board games. The list went on. Some games were meant to be played with partners, others took the solo route. Either way, the options seemed good enough for most of us.

The innocence of youth included the use of language. Swear words were out, period. Using one was cause for concern and punishment. And while I never, ever used profanity in any situation during those years- and for that matter hadn't been introduced to most of them- one particular event that's engrained in my mind happened around that same time period, probably during the winter of 1963 or 64.'

Walking alone and on my way home, I trudged along the border of a foot or more of snow that blanketed the ground. I took the corner of Laurel Avenue and turned for home upon noticing a strange word etched into the snow, likely carved out with a glove or mitten by some local ruffian. Aloud I recited this four-letter word that began with an "F" then headed for home to find out its meaning. It was a new word for sure. Never had I seen it written or used in speech, and wasn't really sure how it was to be pronounced properly. I wanted to impress my father with my expanding vocabulary.

With shoulders back and ready to be congratulated for increasing my vocabulary, I asked him what the heck *fook* meant. My father's reaction and look on his face was the very same I'd seen a thousand times before when I was in trouble. As my body pressed its panic button and my blood pressure began to rise, he didn't hesitate another second. Maybe he'd asked where I'd heard or seen the word, but it mattered not to the outcome. With no chance at all given to explain how I had stumbled across it, subjected I was to an instant punishment and probably a spanking—though I don't recall one. Banished to my room with no opportunity to defend myself at all. It was a valuable lesson learned during such innocent times, and the "F" word unnerves me still to this day.

But the summer months, they ruled. Summer held everything regarding the promise of youth. While toys and games and comic books kept us occupied during the school year and the colder months, it was the magic of summer and all its promise that broke us free, entirely free to explore the world around us. We were set free to wander and ride our bikes and to stay out all day long. And we did just that at nearby Recreation Park.

While we took the variety of splendor the park provided us for granted during those years, we had our choices to make, and many they were. A magnificent carousel was certainly the centerpiece of the park, its herd of wooden painted horses and piped-in organ music imploring us to take a ride. Further down the road a variety of swings, slides and monkey bars were flanked by a decent sized community swimming pool that helped cool us off. Fenced-in tennis courts beyond the adult ball fields, a clubhouse and snack bar, stocked clear to the rafters with candy, gum and baseball cards was positioned perfectly in the middle of it all. Recreation Park certainly offered us everything our little hearts desired. And more.

But the baseball fields we loved most. A massive dirt field split into three playing fields. Though void of grass and laden with rocks and divots, majestic they stood, beseeching us to come on over to play ball. The fields became our neighborhood watering hole, attracting kids from all across the west side of the city. And while the other distractions the park offered kept us busy enough, it was baseball that was by far our biggest outlet. There was never the need to pick up the phone to call friends to play ball, or try gathering enough kids together to support two teams. Recreation Park would take care of that for us, for it served as a magnet drawing in every kid from every neighborhood from every direction, weather permitting.

We'd gather at the fields and choose sides every day, the older boys in charge of the selection process. And there'd be enough players most times to support two entire teams of nine. On rare occasions when less than nine players made up a team, right field remained vacant, any righty sending one anywhere near it was ruled out—shifting the rule for any lefty batter. That single rule forced us to learn timing and waiting for the right pitch.

And from time to time, a girl or two (see Chapter 6) would join in. Of course we'd set restrictions for them. Girls had to be as good as any boy. They had to prove to us their worth on the field, able to throw like boys and be able to do all the things we knew how to do. They had to be able to make instant and sensible decisions required by the laws of baseball. And if they couldn't keep up with us, we lacked the time and patience to teach them the nuances of the game, for games were meaningful. Having even one marginal player on a fully stocked team could lead to its doom. If girls couldn't cut it, they'd be subjected to the sidelines to cheer us on, or off they'd go into the park to do something else.

Gathering the flattest rocks in quick order established the bases and home plate, and searching for ones that were mostly rounded on the edges was not always successful. Pointed edged rocks that could cut through flesh often was all we could find, and on we'd play with little or no regard to any personal safety. Since sliding into bases was both expected and preferred by most of us, likely outcomes included cut knees, shins and arms. But speaking of injury was avoided entirely. We were baseball players. We were supposed to get injured, bruised, cut and sweaty. It's what baseball taught us. Cuts and bruises we'd accumulated became our war wounds, proudly displayed like trophies. We'd show them off and allow the scars to do the talking for us. Deeper respect was given to those with more cuts and bruises accumulated from these baseball wars. Despite the fact a tear or two was shed every now and then, there were no quitters. It wasn't allowed unless a bone was broken or something more serious occurred.

Branded as a quitter was to die a slow and agonizing death, not only in baseball, but in every game. Quitters were labeled as outcasts for future competition, and none of us wanted a quitter on its team. At best, a quitter would be the last kid chosen, forced onto a team by the luck of the draw. Although that harsh reality ruled the day and quitters learned their lessons, I believe it prepared us nicely in facing life's bigger challenges ahead.

One solitary discolored baseball, scuffed and worn, taped multiple times from constant breaking of its seams. One overused ball it was, reliance on any replacement ball centering on the good fortune of finding one left behind or lost by others. Our single source for batting the stuffing out of that ball was in the one bat we'd owned. Dark brown and heavy as a lead pipe, the "Nellie Fox," autographed model was just too long and too heavy for any nine-year old to swing with any reliable outcome. But despite that fact, most of us did learn how to swing and manage its girth. And we did so without complaint. We choked up on the big bat. We swung it early. We made contact more often and with decent results. We took the opportunity to adjust to the circumstances, and managed it well. And as one year turned into another, we grew stronger. The big brown bat felt lighter. It seemed easier to swing. The ball came off the bat faster and reached greater distances than before. We improved our game at differing paces—some just a little and others more enhanced. And while I'd noticed varied transformations in others, my personal progress and maturation accelerated at all levels of the game.

I'd surpassed my peers in everything to do with the game—despite the fact I was the youngest boy on the field. I hit the ball harder and farther than the others. I threw the ball straight and true to its target. I ran down anything hit remotely close to me in the field, and I ran the bases with abandon and conviction. Such a rare hastening of progress had not gone unnoticed by the others. No longer would I languish at the bottom of the order or be one of the last picked on a team. Producing runs and banging homers with regularity meant just one thing—my lowly place in the lineup would need to be changed. And as some of the older boys argued politics at such a preposterous notion, overruled they were by those in charge. Youth and talent would trump status and ego.

So I took my place at the heart of the lineup. Cleanup hitter. A place in the lineup highly revered and recognized holding a responsibility like no other place in the lineup. Production was the key. Clutch hitting and charismatic leadership. And as I took my rightful place in the lineup, I understood there would be challengers. I understood completely the level of expectation would always be greatest as cleanup hitter. And as I bashed homer after homer, my place in the lineup was secured. My reputation was growing in leaps and bounds. And as I grew stronger and continued gaining baseball knowledge, the transformation into Mickey Mantle began taking shape....

So it is these cherished memories I have relived. I've been shown the door to my past and it has opened itself, enabling me to explore its vault. But just as clear as most of these stories have appeared, there is a gray area that is baffling. And because of that, I've taken certain liberties in the telling of this story.

Missing or incorrect names of some boys I'd played with have been replaced with names of others I'd known and grown up with—especially the earlier chapters involving the Binghamton Farm League. Even as my mind has replayed the mysterious clarity of these stories as if they'd just happened, I've been unable to recall the names of some teammates. For that matter, I'm not even sure if standings were kept, or if there'd been team names. As much as I've tried prying them from their hiding places, those particular memories have abandoned me. Although the stories and episodes are as true as I remember them to be, the inability to recall names is perplexing. And for some reason that I can't explain either, my memory for names of players and coaches from the Little League and forward seems to have recovered in full. Names to stories where embarrassing circumstances prevail are purely fictional. I'm sure also that my active and inventive mind has exaggerated and embellished parts of some stories, at least just a little. But they are what my mind chooses to remember—embellished or not.

As I've thought back to when I was Mickey Mantle, fantasizing and longing for the simplicity life offered us kept at me. To go back in time to experience the innocence, camaraderie and competition as seen through dreams was a privilege, one that felt so real to me. I thought about everything Mickey Mantle accomplished on the field of play. The tape-measure homers, the World Series titles, the all-star games, the injuries and missed games—even the baseball cards I had collected and treasured. I thought also of Mickey

Mantle as I learned more about him. I found out what he was really like away from the ballpark and living his life as a real person, not just a ballplayer. In those moments of reflection to alarming facts known of him, one thing was certain. Never had I wavered even a little in my feelings towards him. Oh, I was disappointed and felt somewhat betrayed, even felt pity for him and his family, but never judged him. I felt no need to forgive him for anything he'd felt remorseful about or for the seedy things he had done. Mickey Mantle struggled with life just like most of us. He wasn't the God of baseball like I thought he was. He wasn't some cartoon character who'd never grow old. No, he was made of flesh and blood just like me. And despite admitted character flaws and dark stories revealed about his life, Mickey Mantle remains my hero.

For me, Mickey Mantle was the best there ever was, the best there would ever be, and nothing will change that. I lived for Mickey Mantle and *I lived as* Mickey Mantle during those formative years of my youth. I looked up to him and shared a very special and real connection between us that is most unique. It is a bond that will never be broken, never taken from me no matter how old I live to be. He was there for me when I played baseball, an essence guiding me and challenging me to be the very best I could be. Bob Costas summed it up this way at Mickey's eulogy in 1995, saying, "He was a presence in our lives- a fragile hero to whom we had an emotional attachment so strong and lasting that it defied logic."

For years following Mickey's retirement from baseball, an odd connection between us lived through other Yankee players—Roger Maris, Bobby Murcer, Thurman Munson and Don Mattingly. While Maris played alongside Mickey for many years, he was a close second as my favorite Yankees at the time. I was heartbroken when he went to the Cardinals in 1967, but still I followed his career, keeping him close to my heart as an ex-Yankee.

I hadn't recognized that each of my favorite Yankees last name began with the letter *M,* until having a conversation about baseball with one of my daughters. I'm not sure if Kara or Emily asked me who my favorite Yankees of all-time were, but it took that conversation for me to understand the significance to my answers. My unique connection to Mickey Mantle found an extension through other favorites, subconsciously or not. And I had never given a thought until recently that the last Yankee I truly loved was Don

Mattingly, and that he retired from baseball *the same year* Mickey died. Such a pattern bolsters and confirms what I believe. And as pretentious as it may sound, I take it as a sign.

But a "sign" such as this one is just a prelude to the bigger sign experienced during the summer of 2016. It is the astonishing events experienced in Cooperstown that has enabled me to complete this book, to clear up loose ends and finish this story. That *spiritual experience* has given me my ending—a gift given at just the right time. What happened to me in Cooperstown validated that Mickey is still with me. And as you move from one chapter to another, my hope is that you understand and feel the uncommon bond I share with Mickey Mantle. Even while that experience in Cooperstown may seem unbelievable to some, it is well-chronicled. Published August 25, 2016, the page one issue of, The Cooperstown Crier's, *Making a Pilgrimage To Cooperstown* validates my experience. Oneonta Daily Star editor Sam Pollock not only believed my accounting of what happened that day, but he called it, "One of the best reads of the year." The story of that day, so vital to this story and its climax, is captured in my final thoughts at the end of the book.

I do hope that readers of this book who grew up playing baseball all day and into the night experience the same incredibly strong connection I'd felt during this journey. I hope my memories spent playing baseball as a kid trigger similar memories in you—perhaps not as Mickey Mantle, but as Willie Mays, Duke Snider or any other star player back then. For it is baseball and all it meant to millions of baby-boomers that has illuminated many of our paths. And while we played the game for the fun of it and for the competition, baseball has taught us so much about life itself. There's no denying that. I hope your memories come shining through for you just as mine have for me.

And for those others who'd copied and believed that *they were* Mickey Mantle, very well then. I appreciate that and welcome you to a rather large community. I'm no longer that nine-year old boy coveting the title of Mickey Mantle, believing he had to prove it on the field. I'm willing to share that title these days. Well, maybe just a little.

I believe this story will make you laugh and cry- and hope it does both. My hope also is that it will send you back in time to those magical days of childhood, for it's a story of how childhood heroes fade away as the naivety of childhood passes by. It's a story of revelation, the fragile nature of life and the window of opportunity given in making a difference. It illustrates how heroes have helped shape our lives as discoveries are made. And while decades have past and the longing to be have vanished, there was a time—a very special time indeed—when my name was Mickey Mantle.

2

Imagination

Long before believing I was Mickey Mantle, the power of invention was hard at work within me. Adventure and imagination dominated my naïve and innocent life during the early and mid 1960's. In fact, imagination was my best friend. Certainly I had my fair share of flesh and blood friends—they were all over the neighborhood. But dreaming up and living it out beckoned me at all times, shadowed me at all times. Inborn ability to conjure, invent and imagine was no more than a moment away, a millisecond away. Honed skills in turning it on became as easy as breathing. Instant transformation into anything or anyone I desired to be was on call.

Crafted through multiple experiences, my power was followed by the most terrifying assignments and significant missions known to man. Routinely encountering fierce battles against mankind from every dark corner of the world became my duty. Positioned and known as the highest commander the world had ever known, these secret tasks placed me into precarious situations with improbable endings. Instant transformation worked always, thrusting me into numerous escapades filled with vital importance, fully loaded with edge-of-your seat drama. Drama that far and above exceeded any realism that life offered.

Loaded with danger, deadly projects they were, a veritable potpourri of life-threatening assignments against the evil armies of the world and shrewd bank robbers. Add in cunning villains, ugly thugs from the pages of our comic books, even the ghosts and goblins that lurked outside or even in our bedroom closets or underneath our beds. It mattered not which deadly inferno would be next on the list. For early in this risky existence, I answered the call to conquer evil, often singlehandedly. Protection and honor became my lot in life. Restoring all that was good in the world, protecting and rescuing the innocent and frail, leading the forces of good against the worst enemies. A reputation and resume like no other in the history of the world defined me.

Revolving as the centerpiece to such dangerous missions came countless victory parades and collective thanks from the four corners of the world. Epic quests and conquests against all odds followed me wherever trouble brewed. Battling superior armies outnumbering mine 100 to one became routine. Just show me where they were hiding! To bravely enter the secret woods on the far side of Recreation Park where mortal men dared not venture before. Ha! Take a back seat Mr. Danger, for it was mere child's play. To walk where the brave dare not go? Yes, yes and more yes's, for I would have chosen to march into hell for a heavenly cause had I been called upon by the highest power of all.

No greater power on earth possessed by any man or boy could be found. Harnessed and deployed, this mighty power belonged to me. Clearly I understood assignments and duties, carrying them out humbly and reverently whenever summoned. Inborn ability to transform into any character came in an instant, on call and ready for action.

The Bat Signal flashes across the Gotham City skyline, *I'm Batman*. Meteorites have broken through the atmosphere and bearing down on earth. *I'm Superman*. Thousands of German soldiers are marching upon my fine city and the largest party of Plains Indians has surrounded our encampment. Worry not, and fear not either, dear world, for I am your Supreme Commander.

They say the British are attacking our frozen men at Valley Forge? Move over George Washington, and make way for a new leader in town. A massive party of 5,000 Sioux warriors has my 200 men surrounded at the Little Big Horn. Hmm, take a seat George Custer, and take some notes while you're at it, for I will change the mighty course of history with the most heroic tactics ever before witnessed, saving your fortunate hides as a bonus.

Perfectly I had trained my mind, able to transform everything at my disposal into something other than what it really was. Whatever was available to become what was needed to fulfill my destiny was routine. Hundreds of pennies released from a full coin jar from the kitchen became an army of thousands. Spilled then rolled onto the carpet of our living room floor, coins were organized. Those few turned heads side-up serving as commanders, the remainder as soldiers. Perfectly formed into single-file marching rows I'd align them, an undulating army stretching for miles across the carpet. Marching orders would be presented, and I'd inch the coins forward across that carpet towards a hiding enemy. Nothing more than coins, yet my imagination converted them into two-inch plastic Civil War soldiers and Revolutionary armies I'd seen advertised on the back cover of my comic books. Coins and other props were transferable, for the power was in me to do so. Only an instant away from becoming any army I could imagine.

As Supreme Commander, enormous responsibility fell upon my shoulders. Orders needed to be followed precisely without provocation, inciting men into action for just and righteous causes. Speeches delivered decisively motivated them to lay it on the line. The world would repay them soon enough for such valor. Regarded and remembered they'd become, thousands of battle-tested heroes with little regard for self, sacrificing themselves for me and the world they'd vowed to protect. My powerful words certainly would be inscribed in the great Hall of Records for current and future soldiers needing inspiration, a giant book full of the best quotes ever spoken.

Deep into the heart and soul of every man and beast on the field of combat penetrated words of gold. Leading the charge with proven bravery, my forces charged into uncharted waters of gallantry, letting on no sign of fear or wavering whatsoever. Outnumbered by thousands and lacking proper ammunition and resources to conquer or to compete, enemies stood confounded as our lines moved forward. Certainly outlandish tactics such as these seemed imprudent, but intimidated we were not. That surrendering would soon follow with lopsided casualties and horrific loss of life seemed inevitable. And it was—only we were the victors.

But realism started to matter. I ached for much more. Coins and other props were losing their appeal. Preference to the plastic toy soldiers resonated within me. Despite the fact I'd trained myself to respect them and understood what they'd meant to our relationship, it was time to abandon such simplicity. Badly I needed to graduate higher upon the next level of pretend. Needing that army of plastic soldiers was playing upon my nerves, coveting it now more than any toy I had owned or desired. And as summer turned to spring and spring into fall, something truly wondrous happened. The giant Sears and

Roebucks Christmas catalog found its way into our home just before Thanksgiving.

Particularly appealing were two toys I'd seen advertised on commercials and in newspapers, and I couldn't live without either. Both were splashed across the pages of the Sears and Roebucks Christmas catalog, beckoning and teasing me to come inside its pages and take them home. Unique thinking would be needed, and acquiring one or both toys would be difficult if not improbable. But the pure timing of its arrival couldn't have been better. My ninth birthday was falling on Thanksgiving Day of 1964, and a big party was planned at our house for it. With my friends invited, how perfectly aligned it seemed! I had it all figured out. One for my birthday, the other at Christmas.

Everything any of us ever wanted seemed to be within its cataloged pages. Toys displayed orderly with vivid colors whetting my appetite for more. Bicycles and games positioned perfectly throughout its shiny pages. It was stock full of everything and incredibly thick and heavy—heavier than even the telephone book. I turned those pages and memorized the page numbers of the toys I'd longed for, then folded the corners over for good measure.

Every day I returned religiously to gawk at the two pages. The rapid-fire, multi-functioning weapon Johnny Seven OMA (One Man Army) was first in line. Built with seven distinct functions, the Johnny Seven was set apart from other toy rifles or guns we'd owned and shared. As Supreme Commander, it was crucial to the order that I be the first—and perhaps the only boy to acquire one. With a resume consisting of grenade launcher, anti-tank rocket, armor piercing shells, anti-bunker missiles, repeating rifle, Tommy gun and automatic pistol, the Johnny Seven *One Man Army* was perfectly named.

Several pages away, the 230 piece, *Fort Apache* set beckoned me more. Seemingly so incredibly realistic, its two-inch high soldiers and Indians were posed for war. Loaded with plastic soldiers and Indians, horses and wagons, ramparts, walls and lookout towers, Fort Apache *was* more realistic looking than any toy I'd owned. Soldiers and Indians colored blue and red provided the most realistic look there could be. Wooden walls painted as brown as the timber they'd been cut from featured uneven pointed tips highlighting the natural look of an 1870's fort. Imagining myself in charge of the blue soldiers was the easy part, my brave men repelling and thwarting every valiant charge by the red savages. Gazing upon that page turned my mouth to cotton, my eyes to saucers, my breathing enhanced. Simply I could not imagine my life without either toy.

Changing into and becoming any hero had limitations. Lacking superpowers to convert the Sears catalog into something real was way out of my league. Try as I might, results hadn't changed and dealing with this quandary frustrated me. Powers I had relied upon and taken for granted had distinct barriers. A weapon with seven functions, soldiers and Indians were nothing more than photos on beautifully illustrated pages. Listening with an imaginative ear, the voices and pleas from the soldiers and Indians begged for release. Confinement within those pages had grown to desperation and I understood how badly they needed to be released from their paper incarceration. Unearthly tactics that worked quite well for me in the past were simply no match in this game. Subtle hints would be the answer.

Releasing a tried and true scheme upon my parents in a concentrated manner was the plan. Strategy and follow-up would be the keys needed for an inevitable outcome to my finest hour. Beginning at the catalog seemed reasonable enough. Leaving just those two pages of the Sears catalog open in full view on the dining room table or on a counter in the kitchen was a brilliant idea. Repetitiveness would follow. Surely this approach would work on them, it just had to. They'd catch on soon enough, I was certain of that.

With just a few days before my birthday, some time remained for my parents to purchase at least one of my favorites. The timing of it all was entirely seamless. The big party planned at the house with the boys from the neighborhood would be the perfect time to showcase my plunder. After all, everything filtered through me as their Supreme Commander. Purposely I delayed mailing my Christmas list to Santa, waiting for my birthday to see which one I'd receive first. Revised several times, my Santa's wish-list contained more cross outs and scribble marks than from any paper I'd drawn on before. Formulating one into an unblemished final draft to Santa would be no problem. I'd write either, *FORT APACHE* or, *THE JOHNNY SEVEN OMA* in large dark letters at the very top of the list. Of course I'd need to circle and highlight my greater needs—just in case the big guy didn't understand how important this absolutely was to me. What a win-win situation I found myself in. Nothing could go wrong with this master plan.

On the day of the party, the usual cake and ice cream preceded traditional opening of gifts. Although we played some party games and had loads of fun, I couldn't keep my mind from thinking about the big gift of the day. In usual order, I'd opened the gifts from the boys first, tearing into jigsaw puzzles, comic books, coloring books and board games like a human shredder. Fine gifts indeed, but my focus remained on the bigger prize.

But it seemed as if all the gift giving had concluded. Earlier I'd opened a Civil War color by numbers kit from my parents, but they acted as if that was it. Aftermath of partying ensued. Shredded paper from the gifts had been stuffed into a garbage bag and plates and cups cleared from the table. Accelerated breathing was what I recall. Devastated was an understatement. But as the boys made their way down the hallway towards the door, I heard, "*A Johnny Seven OMA!*" shouted from the lips of my friend, Richard Cahill. Commotion and chaos replaced calm and order. Parting the line of boys standing shoulder-to-shoulder in his way, my father broke through to the front, facing me with a large box in hand. *JOHNNY SEVEN OMA* was written across the giant box. Captioned and illustrated explanations of its multi-functions inscribed in detail and with great color. I opened the box and removed the parts slowly from its packaging, but couldn't wait to see it assembled and ready for action. Carefully we placed that amazing weapon upon its tripod, positioning and examining its huge arsenal of parts.

At that moment I felt something greater and far different than anything before. Words could not explain the utter elation enveloping me. I was on top of the world and over the moon in my make-believe world. And with my army of boys able to see for themselves what was mine, well, things just couldn't get any better. While the boys had no reason to justify abandoning me ever, this gift sealed the deal. Disintegration of armies was inevitable, but not mine. Enhanced my title became, and as I marveled at my new toy and feeling the rare beauty of promotion, I knew beyond the shadow of a doubt the boys would remain under my charge forever.

Snapping out of my reverie, we took it outside. Grenades and anti-tank rockets launched high and far into the sky, followed by testing of remaining weapons. Tried by all in the pecking order of established rank, every component of that magnificent weapon was fired. Range and accuracy was determined. Precision and speed followed. Pretending to be the enemy, several boys took positions against the Johnny Seven to help understand an enemies' point of view. This was crucial and something we'd practiced hundreds of times before. Understanding exactly how The Johnny Seven worked its automated magic gave us an advantage. The Johnny Seven OMA ruled.

Cold weather set in soon enough. Outside we played with the Johnny Seven OMA until the time was right to give it a rest. Johnny Seven was an outdoor toy, and needed to be stored until spring. With that being the facts in the matter, my attention turned to the Fort Apache.

Imagining the Fort Apache on top of Santa's sleigh with my name on its tag continued being my quest. December hit its midpoint, but the days dragged. Sleigh riding and ice-skating at Recreation Park served to pass the time most days, but preoccupation with Fort Apache clouded my mind. Anxiety and nervousness in the matter simply took over. Setting my mind on one purpose for nearly two months weighed me down. The thought of not having that Fort was killing me.

Christmas Eve arrived finally. I tossed and turned all night, replaying my year in review. Would I be getting coal in my stocking? I thought I'd been a pretty good boy that year. Sure, I fought with my two brothers on occasion and didn't clean my room when asked, but these would hardly disqualify me, or would they? I wasn't sure. Santa certainly left the friendly confines of the North Pole by now, on his way somewhere. At this point it was a done deal, there was absolutely nothing I could do but wait. But the waiting game for a nine year old boy at Christmas was the hardest game to play. Sleep was required for this game to play out, but sleep eluded me. My mind was so cluttered there was no way I'd fall asleep.

I imagined where Santa likely was at that very moment. I wondered when he'd come to our house and set that giant Fort Apache box at the foot of the tree. I thought about the cookies and milk we'd left him, and the carrots for his reindeer, then struggled to hear if any of it was being rustled or moved about downstairs. I crawled out from the covers and peaked around the corner landing for any clear signs of him. Impatiently I waited for 10 minutes, then retreated to my room to try falling asleep.

Amidst the mind games swirling in my head, I fell asleep at some point. And when the first rays of sunlight broke through the windows, my brothers and I bolted downstairs as fast as we could, eyes as wide as saucers and our little hearts beating like drums. Our parents emerged from their bedroom, yawning and stretching, but we paid little attention to them, for our collective focus was on that great big tree, and the gifts from Santa that were underneath it.

Scanning the huge cache of gifts surrounding the tree like a wagon train awaiting an Indian attack, I looked carefully for the square Fort Apache box. Distracted by multi-colored ribbons, bows and wrapping paper, I tried focusing. From left to right and up and down my eyes rotated like a berserk ball in a pinball machine. Gifts by the hundreds lay before us! Boxes of all sizes, colors and shapes! My mouth went dry, my hands became clammy, my heart pounded faster than a speeding bullet! Where was my Fort Apache?

My brothers hadn't waited for me to start opening presents. Assaulting the first set of packages like a pack of wolves at the carcass of a fresh kill, green and red wrapping paper flew across the room. Excited shouts of utter joy rang through the air with every box opened. As the real estate of the floor filled with toys and games, only a few gifts remained underneath the tree.

It was then I spotted the largest package of all, and my name was on it. Wasting no time, my greedy little hands shredded the paper like no other boy in the history of boys had done before. I tore the last few scraps of paper from the box, pulled it onto my lap and read the two most beautiful words my young mind ever read before. *Fort Apache*. Thick staples fastened to each corner of the box slowed me down. My fingers pulled the staples but they were too thick and sharp and wouldn't give. My father retrieved a tool from the kitchen to remove the staples. Angst was killing me. Eternity followed as one staple fell off, then another and another. The lid was removed, releasing my new army to the world, and they seemed eager and ready to meet their new commander, *Commander Gary Kaschak*.

Packaged neatly in plastic bags, I spotted the red Indians and blue soldiers. Ripping the bags apart, I set out at once to line them up on the very rug the pennies once roamed. That action signaled graduation into a new level of pretend, a new level of fantasy.

• • • • •

Where armies of pennies once roamed the wilderness and conquered the world, two-inch, plastic men replaced them. They stood perfectly in fighting poses and stances, ready for me to take them to what they had been born to do.

Fantasies like those continued with everything in my young life. Wooden legs of my bed became a hiding place for the little plastic Indians, an air gun received the following Christmas used to blast them away. Injured and bleeding in the mountains above them and with no help from the outside coming for days, I'd pick them off, one by one. They'd fly across the room as the air hit them square in the middle of their plastic bodies, bulls-eye shooting each and every time. Ruffled covers of that same bed became hills and mountains for others to take refuge in. Plastic swords or toy guns became real swords and guns. I morphed into more characters than could be expected in a hundred lifetimes, nay a thousand! I was Batman, battling the Riddler, Joker and Penguin to save Gotham City from their diabolical schemes against the world. Minutes later I'd change to the Commanding General of the Union army. My mind wandered often and free into the ever-growing make-believe world I was called upon to protect.

But as age nine became 10, my mind took a sudden turn into a newer and more exciting world of make-believe, and that was baseball.

Years earlier, our father introduced me and my older brother John to the ball fields of Recreation Park, situated no more than a stones- throw from our front porch. Basic training facilities such as these enabled us to hone our emerging baseball skills, and in the summer of 1960, at the ripe old age of four-and-a-half, the art of hitting, catching, fielding and running the bases became our summer fun.

Good weather or a little rain, it mattered not. We learned how to slide and hit the cutoff man and to understand the game and its beautiful intricacies, position by position. We became students of the game, learning situational baseball in every facet of play. Dad pushed us to learn, understand and utilize information to extend our knowledge to the finer parts of the game. Far ahead of any other neighborhood kid, we hit, ran and fielded the ball repetitively until we became good players. Terrific players.

Learning the game and playing it as often as we did converted us naturally into following and becoming fans of the New York Yankees. The mighty Yankees became baseball's version of Superman, winning American League pennants during my formative baseball-loving years of 1960-64. Consistency of performance by the Yankees during those years and earlier had been taken for granted by the baseball world, as it had by me. Representing the AL in the World Series seemed as automatic as a Mickey Mantle home run. Certainly the World Series would feature the Yankees as the AL representative every year until the end of time. Or that's how it seemed.

Our sudden love for baseball began a transformation in me. Turning away from plastic soldiers and comic book heroes had begun. My interest in the game and its past heroes and top teams took over. As I learned about the history of baseball, I received from Santa a new toy replacing Johnny Seven, Fort Apache and air gun as my favorite. Allowing me to escape into another realm of fantasy, this new toy occupied my time for years on end (and still own!). It was a board game called, *All-Star Baseball*.

Circular cards full of Hall of Fame players were placed on a spinner, 14 numbers spaced apart indicating everything from strikeouts to walks, singles to home runs, groundouts to fly ball outs. Playing All-Star Baseball led to understanding basic statistics of the game, every number having meaning. The concept of the game allowed for solo play, so I took advantage of rainy days, snowy days, even the best of days, to pull that game out from underneath my bed and bring its characters to life. Converting reality into make-believe felt still within my grasp. I formed new baseball leagues, choosing rosters randomly from names inside the pages of the local phone book. Flipping through pages then landing randomly on any page, I'd point to a name and assign that "player" to a team. I'd fill a team roster with 25 names to teams like the *Milwaukee Mashers* or the *Birmingham Bunters*. I'd schedule league games, and despite my age, I was conscious of geography, road-trips and home stands, taking into account the logistics needed in scheduling games.

Trades, injuries and fantastic games and comebacks occurred, just like in real baseball. Standings and league leaders were posted daily. While studying basic algebra was still several years away, understanding wins and losses and calculating games behind seemed fairly simple. I hadn't learned how to calculate batting averages or winning percentages, so I studied statistics posted in the Sunday paper, "rounding up" most of the time, occasionally finding an exact match to a player or team.

The league was my fantasy league. I was commissioner, scheduler, general-manager and scout, in charge of everything, just the way I preferred. And it didn't end with baseball. I used those disks for other sports, following a similar routine with pro football, basketball, hockey and even bowling. I'd invented new leagues and team names for very sport there was, stretching the limits of my imagination. I began memorizing basis statistics and winning percentages, and to this day—because of All-Star Baseball—calculating and understanding basic mathematical formulas has come easy to me.

• • • • •

But baseball remained my favorite sport. I couldn't wait for a baseball season to begin and to root for my heroes, my New York Yankees. We had a natural love and attraction to the Yankees. Binghamton was Yankees country, and our minor league Binghamton Triplets team was affiliated, supplying the big club ample talent at just the right time in any season. Players like Bobby Richardson, Whitey Ford, Tom Tresh and Joe Pepitone played for our Triplets, filling us with a sense of pride watching local guys swinging and pitching for our beloved Yankees. And we'd learned of the Yankees mostly from the televised games on Sunday afternoon—the one day during the week when games were telecast. We'd take that day to learn about our heroes, what they looked like, the positions played, how they ran the bases. We'd listen intently to announcers giving out-of-town scores, updating us on league standings and more. Through the games we became incredibly attached to our team, motivating us to start collecting baseball cards—always on the lookout for any Yankee player.

While baseball cards began filling our pockets and shoe boxes with players from every team, the most sought after cards seemed to be missing from just about every pack of cards. And so it went with coveted star players from other teams. Al Kaline, Rocky Colavito, Willie Mays, Hank Aaron and a host of others. As much as we'd hoped and prayed for any star player to be inside our next pack of cards, far and away the Mickey Mantle card was the one most kids looked for.

I loved Mickey Mantle. Easily he became my newest and greatest hero, surpassing Batman, Superman, and Supreme Commander. When I opened a pack of cards for what seemed to be the millionth time and a Mickey Mantle card appeared, I lost my mind. I was elated and relieved and could hardly believe my eyes. Proudly, I placed my Mantle card inside the crown of my baseball cap, and when I unwrapped a second Mantle card, I wedged it between spokes of my bike. Both positions were reverent symbols of where the best deserved to be, who was most admired and respected. Little did we know at the time that our actions would deflate a cards value. But we weren't collecting for profit. We were collecting for status.

And so I copied Mickey's batting stance, ran the bases like him and tried switch-hitting. In short order, I grew from liking Mickey Mantle into *becoming Mickey Mantle.*

Calling upon instructions my father taught us enabled me to get really good at baseball. He pitched thousands of balls, tossed thousands more in the air and hit thousands more to us in the field. But as long and as often as we'd repeat those three things into the early evening hours, we never felt bored. I loved every second of baseball. There was nothing about the game I didn't enjoy. The process was like no other sport, and I soaked it up like a sponge. We took what we'd learned and headed to the ball fields at nearby Recreation Park for some much needed competition.

Void of grass and sod, the all dirt playing fields were in line once the whiffle-ball we'd played at the Horace Mann schoolyard didn't seem enough anymore. Where the Horace Mann playground was blacktopped, Recreation Park was all dirt. Where a foul ball would land in the street, now it was playable. Where a home run would (sometimes) hit the Barrett's house, or even bust a window (done that) now it could be caught. Where a fall on the pavement resulted in skinned-knees, we were free now to slide at will. What a perfect setting to prove to the world that I was Mickey Mantle.

That experience and repetition served me well. As one home run after another left my golden bat and sailed into the next county, it was apparent I was closing in on the coveted home run title. Through all the battles with the other boys, I was winning by attrition. With Mantle-like regularity, I did my job, and did it better than any other boy in the neighborhood—even the older boys. As I continued an onslaught against defenseless baseball's, abundantly clear it became. I clubbed so many home runs they stopped counting, for it was a number never before reached. No one knew how many, but it had to be more than a thousand. The number was so high that keeping track seemed irrelevant. The record was mine and always would be mine, something so etched in stone and so out of reach by any mortal man. I was Mickey Mantle, the greatest player of all time.

But that's truly beside the point here. I was born for greatness, born to lead. I wasn't just pretending to be Mickey Mantle anymore when coming to the plate to whack another homer, to pump up the Yankee Stadium crowd, and to win the game singlehandedly. No, indeed! I had convinced myself that *I was Mickey Mantle*, the greatest player of all! Yes, my name was Mickey Mantle, born November 26, 1955 at Our Lady Of Lourdes Hospital in Binghamton, New York.

3

The Concussion Game: My First Game

My first steps in tasting organized baseball came during the summer of 1964 in the form of the Binghamton Farm League. As an eight-year old going on nine, it would have to be the lowly minor leagues for now, and while I felt I was good enough or even better than most of the older boys playing Little League, it would have to do.

I'd prove myself in probably just a game or two, perhaps even as little as a swing or two. Showing coaches from other teams I was ready to compete at such a level was what my mind was set on proving. Unable they would be to overlook the distances of my home runs, strength of my arm and the finesse and wisdom in how I played and managed myself in any one game. How could they discriminate against me, Mickey Mantle, simply because of my age? Had not the word travelled far and wide of my baseball exploits displayed on the pavement of the Horace Mann schoolyard and the fields of Recreation Park? Had I not proven to Binghamton that I had perfected myself into the best ballplayer the game had ever witnessed? Patience in the matter would be required, but patience was a difficult concept to manage for any nine-year-old baseball player. So I vowed to hit the stuffing out of the ball each and every time an opposing hurler faced me. I'd keep them on their toes and nervous to face me every time I strode to the plate. That was the master plan.

With the majority of games played on the dirt fields we'd grown accustomed to, a great advantage existed in knowing the particulars of each field. Familiarity and knowledge of every nook and cranny had been categorized in my mind for safekeeping. The short distance to left of field one, the spaciousness in the outfield of field two, and the sloping bank in left of field three. These very fields where we used rocks for bases and one taped-up, battered old ball and broken bat had transformed into fields of real bases, shiny white baseballs and a multitude of bats in all sizes and weights. Scorebooks and coaches and volunteer umpires were everywhere. To get on that field and get the first game of my minor league career started had arrived!

Invigorating energy and chaos persisted on the fields as players began warming up. Kids were scattered in unorganized groups, looking around for some sort of guidance from the coaches as to what to do. I felt anxious and loaded with butterflies, but decided to make the first move. With an eye on a kaki-green equipment bag nearby, I forged towards it, focusing completely on one ashen-colored bat standing out from the others. Imagining my name written across its label, confidently I began a John Wayne-like stride towards it. Others took my lead and paired up to play catch. A few more dug into a second equipment bag and began taking practice swings. Some boys tried on the wobbly blue helmets that fit none of us properly, while others broke into groups to play pepper. Everything I wanted my first game to be seemed just right. It all seemed so perfect. Baseball was alive. It was singing to us.

Distractions often altered my focus, and my focus was on that bat. Picturing what awaited the world after taking my first swing came to mind. Long and far the ball would ascend, arching so high and so far that where it landed likely would be in the next county. Jaws dropping from the mouths of everyone as the ball flew out of sight, a look of awe and envy from every kid on every team. I imagined myself carried off the field following the game, my initial homer just a prelude of things to come. As such glorious thoughts came to mind, I reached for the bat.

What happened next did cause me to be carted off the field. Not from hitting a home run or making a great catch in the field. Not a great throw from the outfield, or a steal of home to seal the win for my team. *Unusual* caused me to be carted off the field, likely the first time in baseball history. So unusual that it would likely provide lasting memories to any player or coach witnessing it firsthand.

About to reach for the bat and oblivious to everything going on around me, I pulled down the rim of my cap, cocky and defiant. That particular bat was going to feel great nestled around my strong hands. Contrasting visibly with sun-toned arms of steel, its ashen color would stand out nicely. And as I began pulling that beautiful bat from the bag, down I went hard, sinking to the ground as if knocked out by some sucker punch from the side.

As if I'd just finished a whirling ride at a carnival, the world spun rapidly. I lay motionless on my back, confounded by the inability of my body to move. The coaches rushed over. Lips and mouths moved, but understanding this gibberish seemed impossible, this foreign language not registering. Tears bubbled up in my eyes and I tried clearing them, but my Popeye-like arms turned to rubber, useless and dead. My head continued spinning like a top, my vision blurred, and the headache of all headaches pounded like a storm. I was puzzled, confused and scared, and wondered what the heck just happened. Had an errant ball hit me? Had a car run me over? Had I suffered a heart attack at such a young age? I had no idea what caused my body to shut down so abruptly. And as the horrible dizzy spell continued its dance, memories from just a year ago came back to me in a rush.

Unintentionally, I had been conked in the head the previous summer by a flying horseshoe. That's right—a flying horseshoe. While its intended target stood 40 feet away staked to the ground, the throw was not an errant one. It hadn't slipped at all from the man sending it on its course. What was errant and out of place was me. A neighborhood game of horseshoes played by men at a party had been going on for the better part of the day. But while the men competed against each other, there were other games at play on that same field—life and death games.

Squaring off against an evil boy standing 40 feet away, a gunfight to the death began. We began the slow march forward. With plastic guns tucked inside holsters, we inched our way towards each other, inevitable that just one would survive the upcoming shootout. With a reputation as the fastest gun in the west, my opponent had slayed dozens of others in similar contests. Word was that he was faster than anything anyone witnessed before. Faster than lightning was the word on the street.

Intimidated I was not. Never would I be. Words and rumors never scared me, and he was challenging me. He'd heard I was the fastest gun around- even faster than he was- and any bragging-rights to such a claim was reserved for just one. But I hadn't bragged about it like he had—it wasn't my style. My job was to serve and protect—that was it. And while he mowed down one lawman after another in his evil pursuit of greatness and legend, the good and all I stood for was reason enough to oblige the challenge. There was no way I would lose to him. Good over evil prevailed at such times.

Lining up along the street, townsfolk gathered to watch. They huddled close enough to hear our words, yet far enough away to remain out of harms way. Gently I gnawed at a toothpick, then reached down to open the flap of my holster, slow and easy. I tossed what remained of the toothpick away and looked sharply into his evil eyes, continuing forward. In seconds, the space between us was just about right- only a few more paces before the proper time to draw our guns. And as that time came and we went for our guns, down I went in a heap.

• • • •

At the time I hadn't known what it felt like to be shot. Previous gunfights were make-believe. But as I buckled over and sank to the ground, I wasn't sure what happened. Had this hooligan pulled the trigger of a real gun with a real bullet? Had I *really* been shot, and was I going to die? My impressionable mind led to that conclusion. But what else would I be thinking at such a time? We had just drawn guns and down I went. And my head was ringing as if sirens were going off around me. I was scared, that was for certain. I didn't deserve to die in such a manner, my final moments on earth spent on the ground next door to my house.

Several men rushed to my aid, circling me like vultures and speaking words I couldn't understand or follow. My head kept spinning and I couldn't focus my eyes on anything. They examined me roughly, turning me onto my stomach and then turning me over again like some piece of meat on a grill. I started understanding a few words, feeling a bit relieved that I hadn't been shot by the other boy. That's when I spotted a horseshoe next to me on the ground and it started making sense. One man said I'd likely suffered a concussion and others agreed. I had never heard the word before, but it sounded bad- just not bad enough for them to send me off to the hospital- a unanimous decision. And as the waves of concussion reverberated throughout my brain, I was yanked from the ground by a few of the men then taken briskly to the side yard and away from the action. I could barely walk and still couldn't focus my eyes properly. At least three of everything was altering my view of the world, and nothing at all seemed proportional. As the minutes went by and some vision returned gradually, it became apparent what happened.

While the epic gunfight battle had been fought in a north to south direction, the horseshoe game played east to west. The perfect crisscross for such a brutal accident made possible by my single-mindedness in shutting out everything around me.

. . . . .

Those were my thoughts as I lay on the ground of the baseball field. The pain and rapid patterns of dizziness felt no different than those experienced after being clocked by that horseshoe, and the language spoken by the coaches hovering over me was no different, either. I had no idea I'd wandered unintentionally into the space where another boy was taking practice swings. It was a small circle of space we'd been taught to respect and avoid crossing at all times, and breaching it was not allowed and unsafe to enter. I had no idea that accident would be one of several unusual injuries I'd suffer both on and off the field—weird injuries that seemed to plague me for years. Much as injuries were all part of the game, the bad ones could keep a player out of the lineup, and I wasn't about to let it happen to me now.

But learning what I had about Mickey Mantle's injuries—especially banged-up knees requiring hours of taping and setting prior to each and every game—seemed to bring me that much closer to him. Truly this stood out as one of the reasons he was my all-time hero, and a great reason to look up to him. Selfless and determined he was, with intestinal fortitude like no other in the history of fortitude. Mickey Mantle was able to battle against the odds, to pull himself together like the great hero he was, and to rise from the ashes-no matter what injury he sustained. A hero unlike all others was Mickey Mantle, leading his Yankee club to another victory, another American League pennant, another World Series appearance.

As my mind whirled and a horrible nausea set in, the coaches pulled me onto my feet and the muffled words they spoke began making some sense. Strange buzzing inside my head increased and magnified- no different than the sound the horseshoe produced. I'm sure I looked like a drunk as they walked me to the side of the field and ordered me to sit down. Dispassionately they instructed me to hold a block of ice against my head, then performed what best could be described as a cursory check of my faculties. When I'd given them a few answers to some simple questions, they'd surmised somehow that I'd be just fine. Unanimously the decision to let me sit and rest had been made, with no need to see a doctor or rush to the hospital for anything precautionary. And since I hadn't visited a doctor after the horseshoe incident, I was good to go. No longer did anyone seem overly concerned for me. And as they walked away following the second concussion I'd endured in just a year's time, I still had no idea what really happened to me. I pressed the ice down against my neck and waited for whatever was going to happen. There was a game to be played and I was going to play in it—concussion or not.

The boy who'd smacked my head approached me and explained the whole thing. He'd assumed there was a significant clearing around him and hadn't noticed me coming towards him. While others implored me to stop walking, I kept going. One boy tried warning me by pulling on my arm, but on I went, paying no attention to any warnings from anyone. I wasn't upset at him. Nothing he had done was intentional. Heroes knew how to take such things in stride and how to react under adverse conditions. Preparing and reacting properly was what made us different. I shook his hand and that was that.

Cobwebs began fading away and my eyes regained partial focus. Drawing upon qualities of greatness and leadership was needed *right now*. I needed to prove to the coaches that I was ready to play, that recovery time for me was far less than that of the average boy. Tossing the useless ice pack down on the ground and feeling a renewed sense of purpose and vigor, I stormed towards the coaches. Tugging on the shirtsleeve of our coach, I stated defiantly, "I'm ready to play ball. I'm feeling good."

I thought he'd be impressed at my rapid and unprecedented recovery, but he wasn't. Instead, he frowned as if it had been the dumbest remark he had ever heard. My body straightened and I repeated my claim. He didn't waver.

Looking away to avoid eye contact for some reason, he said, "Already made out the lineup, kid. Maybe I'll get you in later. Let's see how it goes."

The thought did not sit well with me. And why would it? After all, I had played ball each and every day leading up to this opening day, practicing and contemplating all of it. Mammoth home runs belted on the schoolyard of Horace Mann School and on this very field of Recreation Park had become routine. Anticipating opening day during all that time had been what I lived for—a springboard to future days playing in the Little League and onto Yankee Stadium needed to begin right here. Leapfrogging my way to stardom in the shortest period of time was my destiny, and all of it was supposed to begin here on opening day. This was not supposed to happen.

So I thought about Mickey again and wondered what he would have done in such a pickle. Drawing upon his greatness and leadership, it felt as if Mickey was speaking to me telepathically, reminding me that this was my destiny. Calming me down, he asked for patience, instructing me to prepare myself for setbacks such as this one, that the world would know soon enough of what I was made of. Time, he said, would take care of everything. As I thought it all over, my team took the field without me.

Slumping away, I took to the sidelines and watched them register three quick outs. Our first official at bat was next, and as jealousy swept through my veins, a new set of tears streamed down my face. I tried hiding them but couldn't. It just wasn't fair. Suggestions from Mickey weren't working very well. Understanding the patience required to get through this dilemma was near impossible to grasp or agree to. Coach said he'd try getting me into the game, but that wasn't good enough, wasn't what I expected. Centerfield was where I belonged, and batting cleanup in the lineup. Pinch-hitting and getting into the game as a substitute was embarrassing. I couldn't take it, couldn't stand the thought of not playing every inning of the game. Bitter and resentful I felt listening to the lineup being read. And as the innings whizzed by and the game grew shorter, I felt alone and out of place, wondering if coach would really try getting me into the game.

Staying fresh and loose was important and kept me believing that I'd get in. Between innings I'd play catch with a few boys on the bench and take cuts on the side when we were in the field. Surely during those times opposing coaches studied my graceful swings and impeccable timing—performed with the composure of a superstar. They had to have noticed something, were likely relieved I hadn't been in and wondering why that was. But as the innings passed and the score remained tied, the signal I looked for hadn't come. Never had I felt worse as the third, fourth and fifth innings came and went. Depression turned to sulking. Hope to despair. And with not even a cursory look from our coach, I sensed there was no chance I'd get in. I felt defeated.

The score remained tied into the final inning, and I'd managed somehow to keep hope alive. Studying the lineup and running his hand down his chin, coach seemed to be at odds with himself. Big Bobby was our scheduled batter, and that mortified me. He had no concept or plan and struck out every time earlier, not bothering to swing even once. There the bat sat on his shoulder as if he were posing for pictures, and helping him on the bench between innings had done nothing to change his statue-like plate appearances. I'd demonstrated proper techniques in holding a bat and when to swing it, but baseball mechanics and science only confused him.

· · · · ·

Despite multiple attempts, there seemed little or no hope for him. His girth and clumsy mannerisms went against him, and the only decent quality Bobby had was the size of his grin, rivaled by the size of his body. Grinning was what he did best. Striking out always never altered his annoying expression, as if he'd enjoyed striking out. That was most difficult to come to grips with, for why bother being on a team if effort, guts and determination hadn't been important. If we were going to win games, Bobby had to improve, and that went without saying. But I knew he'd strike out again, and hoped beyond hope that coach would send me in to pinch-hit for him now.

Holy cow! Why hadn't our coach noticed what I had noticed from the start! The easiest strikeout in the league was about to bat again while I still languished on the bench! Concussion or not, I needed to bat right now. I'd pictured myself batting in place of Bobby on each of his abysmal at bats, knowing beyond the shadow of a doubt that the game would have been decided had I batted for him even just once. There'd be no way I'd be frozen in fear or afraid to take a swing to win the game. No indeed! I was Mickey Mantle. Born to lead, born to win and born for moments like these.

I looked at coach for the millionth time and realized I was the only player that hadn't played. Even Little Jackie got in before me, striking out as often and as predictable as Big Bobby had. But Little Jackie tried, lunging awkwardly with strange and weak swings. He swung so late it seemed as if he'd been lifting a sledgehammer instead of a baseball bat. And working with him produced similar results to Big Bobby's. Nothing demonstrated seemed to help or even matter. And Little Jackie was quirky and fidgety, an attention span unbecoming of a ballplayer. He had strange eyes that spun around and danced like a top, making it near impossible to look him in the eye. Where Big Bobby smiled the widest smile in the history of smiles, Little Jackie fiddled and moved about. He'd crinkle his nose and turn his eyes in and out in a weird sort of way, and when he was alone he twirled his curly hair as if it was spaghetti. He never seemed to pay attention, and didn't say very much, speaking only a few words that usually made no sense at all to the conversation. This pair of boys had not a clue to what it took to be a baseball player, and there they were playing ahead of me.

As I glared at our coach and wished again for my name to be called, he grabbed the swaying arm of Bobby and told him to take a seat. Coach glanced my way from the corner of his eye and with little inflection or enthusiasm he announced, "Kaschak, grab a bat. You're in for Bobby."

Those were the words I'd longed to hear during those six excruciatingly long innings, and while I had prayed and wished for them to be spoken, I stood like a statue and wondered if he'd really said them. He repeated himself, annoyed and poised to change his mind. I snapped out of my reverie and jammed a wobbly blue helmet over my aching head. I grabbed the bat I'd kept at my side, and when I stepped into the box for my first official at bat of the Binghamton Farm League, I was prepared, focused and ready to end the game with one mighty swing.

I had studied the pitcher during the game. He didn't have much of a fastball- the only pitch any of us knew how to throw. And I knew I could hit him and I'd need just one pitch to end the game. I looked to leftfield and thought, *he's* in *too close*. But it wasn't his fault. He hadn't seen me bat, and being the last player put into the game, I understood. I thought about the hundreds of balls I'd hit on this field during hundreds of pickup games, watching ball after ball disappear over the sloping bank just beyond left. And I knew I was about to do it again—envisioning it a hundred times or more during this very game. I knew also I'd need to prove myself during this at bat, perhaps the most important one in my budding career. The pressure to perform was on.

The first pitch was the only pitch needed. My only swing was perfect and true, a textbook sound of bat meeting ball with a sound like no other. As I watched that long, arching fly ball disappear far beyond the hill in left, I tossed down my bat and began my Mickey Mantle home run trot. With head down and a hobble to my step, I circled the bases at just the right speed, and as I rounded third and headed home, I lifted my head to see what kind of greeting awaited me.

My teammates gathered around the plate, cheering and laughing. The moment my foot touched home, they lifted me up and carried me away. We were winners. My long homer was likely the longest anyone had ever witnessed, the loudest sound ever heard from a batted ball. The glory was mine, just as I had imagined it to be.

I had experienced glorious outcomes as Supreme Commander, Batman and Superman, but this one was way different. It was far more real than make-believe feelings conjured from a make-believe world. It was a euphoria I had not come close to experiencing. For the first time playing ball, I knew what it *really* felt like to be Mickey Mantle.

4

The Busted (Smelly) Sneaker Game

The splitting headache pounded inside my head for days, but I paid little attention to that minor interruption. There were more games to play, more home runs to hit, more accolades to receive from my ever-growing fan base. I wasn't about to let a simple concussion slow me down. No, not a headache, not a cold, not the mumps or measles would keep me off the field I was born to rule and conquer. And as Mickey Mantle, a certain degree of obligation was owed to the fans. Undoubtedly, hundreds if not thousands of patrons would pay good money to watch me play, but for now there would be no charge. Time would take care of the rest.

Game after game I launched homer upon homer, every one clearing the left field bank easily. The bank served as a natural fence to the outfield of field three. Located at the far end of Recreation Park, it became my favorite. I could see the ball better than on the other fields, and the ball seemed to fly with more velocity and height. Other fields had no natural barrier in left, no fences or hills to keep a ball from vanishing from view. I'd enjoyed watching my home runs disappear from sight. A home trot seemed more appropriate than legging one out for an inside-the-parker. Not that I couldn't or hadn't, for I had legged them out dozens of times. With half our games scheduled on other fields, I had given the matter considerable thought, needing to adjust my stroke to each field, to make necessary adjustments to the odd dimensions of each.

My swings had to have come from the Gods. A slight drop of the hands, left foot moving forward, then recoiling like a snake into one graceful motion. Never in the history of swings had one like mine been seen, envied by the likes of Babe Ruth and Joe Dimaggio. I imagined them watching from somewhere, the Babe with tears in his eyes, wondering what he might have become had he duplicated my swing. I'm certain his home run totals would have been out of sight, his 714 surpassing a thousand or more. And Joe Dimaggio wishing he'd met me early in his career, wondering how far his 56 game hitting streak would have extended had I been there teaching him the art of hitting.

But this was my time. Though I'd felt sorry those Yankee greats played before my time, it would be just a matter of time for The Sultan of Swat and the Yankee Clipper to take a back seat to what I would become. I was destined for stardom. I'd hit a few thousand homers, assemble a hitting streak of 112 games and I'd break every record. I was *The Mick*, the best nickname and player in the game. I'd be an all-star every year, the League MVP and Triple-Crown winner and would hold the World Series trophy over my head every October. And when it was all over, a plaque with my name would hang along with Yankee greats at the Monument Park in Yankee Stadium. And of course they'd vote me into the Hall of Fame at Cooperstown, unanimously on the first ballot.

But it was yet to be. There was work to be done. As Mickey Mantle, history would be made every game, with a high degree of responsibility placed on every at bat. I needed to stay on it, to focus and remain patient, the mighty course of baseball history taking shape on these fields. Everything done and accomplished here would be checked off a long list that would catapult me to the next levels of play—levels I knew awaited me.

The home run hit to win our first game had done exactly what I'd wanted it to do. The pressure of that moment and how I'd come through in the clutch had not gone lost on our quirky coach. My rightful place in the lineup was restored and all seemed corrected in the universe. I was batting cleanup, the most prestigious and important batting position in the order offering distinction like no other. Cleanup announced the best hitter, the one most likely to come through when things mattered most. Batting fourth held a position of reverence, power and status, reserved for me long ago.

How had I become qualified for such an important position at my age? It was a question I was certain was asked hundreds of times by the experts. Answers were coming. But I would honor the tradition of those coming before me, respecting accomplishments from past heroes. I'd allow my bat, glove and my wits to tell this new story. I would remain as quiet as a boy in church, keeping all of it inside, for bragging would be unnecessary. Incredible restraint I'd demonstrate, restraint from boasting about what I could do on the field of play. And I'd understood the entire world would be watching every move, listening to every word, and taking notes preparing future generations to remember my contributions to the game.

Then one day, our game was scheduled on a new field, the all grass field of West Junior High School. The fields were nearby, located just beyond the evil woods at the far end of Recreation Park. We drove to the game and parked along the street just above the fields of play. Where there were three fields at Recreation Park, this sprawling facility had room for eight.

There were kids everywhere gathering equipment, listening to coaches and trying to figure out which field they would be playing on. Some pointed and marveled at the shear size of the place, but I focused differently. I scanned the fields with hawk-like eyes, searching for a special field where a long homer could be made. I looked left and right, to the far corners and down the middle. I slowed things down and looked again, but my eyes locked onto the field to my right. It seemed to be the perfect field to play a game, and where I wanted our game to be.

There were sloping banks surrounding the field of play along both sidelines, evenly spaced at both base lines. The base paths had worn down considerably from frequent trampling, as did the outfield grass. I laughed at the distance from home plate to the outfield markers, knew how easy it would be to smack one or two over the head of any outfielder. Doomed they'd be, unable to recover in time to chase down any ball that I'd clobber. I couldn't wait to get the game going.

Coach gathered us around, then pointed and announced, "We play here." I wasted no time responding. I rushed down the steep hill like I had never rushed down a hill before, incredibly eager and full of energy. When I reached the flat ground and got back my breath, I had a feeling this game would be different than any other game we'd played. I had a hunch that somehow I would be right in the middle of things, that I'd have something to do with its outcome, something more sensational than the ending to the concussion game. And I'd be right.

The game was a constant see-saw battle between the top two scoring teams in the league. Runs were being scored in every inning, crooked numbers that ran the score quickly to that of a football game, the lead changing hands after every half inning. Back and forth like two prize-fighters fighting for the championship. There had been more hits, walks, errors and mistakes made in just five innings, and the runs kept on coming—mostly on eight combined home runs with half hit by me.

I'm sure that I'd produced at least a dozen runs batted in as we headed to our last at bat. But we trailed by five run, the odds in catching up or outright winning the game somewhat slim. But we'd come back from five run deficits twice earlier, and felt confident we'd do it again. This was a beginner's league where anything and everything happened. Overcoming a five run deficit could be attained from the next six batters in a matter of minutes, and we were ready for that happening. We'd scored innings of five, six and seven runs, and hadn't scored less than four in any other. Scoring five runs seemed practical. This was our chance to show the world what we were made of, and to stamp our seal on the greatest comeback win in the history of the league.

The other games ended earlier and darkness was settling in. Many of the players from other teams gathered alongside the bank to watch our last at bat, some rooting for us to stage a miracle comeback. But I was certain they were hanging around waiting for a chance to watch me bat again, curious to know who'd hit so many homers interrupting their games. But I was scheduled to bat 8th in the inning, my fourth homer of the game an inning earlier pulling us to within one run until they rallied for a four spot in the sixth. I hadn't imagined hitting four in one game, but I had. For us to have a decent chance to win I'd need to bat again, and that would take some luck. Anything and everything happened in this game, but I wasn't too keen on luck at the moment. Big Bobby and Little Jackie were scheduled ahead of me and neither one progressed since the concussion game. What we needed was a miracle.

But miracle games and opportunities was what I was made for. My little mind couldn't stand knowing what was needed to win the game, that the odds stacked against it from happening were slim. But I picked up a bat and knew to be ready. I rooted mightily for our first two hitters, but they struck out on six straight questionable calls. Six pitches had been thrown in the inning, and from my vantage point each had clearly been way out of the strike zone. This hadn't gone unnoticed by our hot-tempered coach. He yelled at the umpire after every pitch, then mumbled as he often had, uttering parts of words I could not identify, or be allowed to repeat at home. Following the third strike called to our second batter, he erupted like a volcano, blowing his top and letting the ump have it. I recall hearing him ask the ump if he was "Late for dinner," then holding his broken reading glasses out. The umpire didn't seem amused, reacting with a barrage of words bordering on profanity. But when he glanced at his wristwatch prior to slamming his mask over his head, coach didn't like or appreciate it one bit. He stormed towards home plate with eyeglasses in hand, trembling and pointing to his wristwatch and asking the umpire if he had a date. He continued his tirade, emphasizing he was "Blind in one eye and couldn't see out of the other." As they went back and forth in this epic battle, I tried comforting my teammates who had struck out. They hadn't deserved such a fate- striking out on pitches a mile out of the strike zone. But there were tears in their eyes. They knew we'd rallied before, but we were down to our last out, not only battling our opponent but an umpire as well. Such was the luck of the game, I thought. Sure, I had seen bad calls before, but this was the deluxe version. It was terribly obvious what was happening. All seemed lost, and that wasn't the worst of things. Little Jackie and Big Bobby were our next scheduled batters.

I'd tried teaching baseball 101 to both of them during the concussion game, but nothing changed. In this game alone, they'd broken the dubious record for most strikeouts combined by hitters in the history of combined strikeouts. The miracle finish I had anticipated surely wasn't going to happen now. Something greater than a miracle was needed to have a chance at winning this game.

As the boys on the other team recognized Little Jackie approaching home and Big Bobby on deck, they relaxed and started intimidating chants to help rattle and unnerve them. But it wasn't necessary. Never had I witnessed such utter failure from such a pair. Where I had succeeded with homer after homer, these two misfits distinguished themselves with strikeout after strikeout, hardly even taking a swing at any pitch, as if they had been born to strikeout.

The opposing coach directed his players in the outfield to come in as far as they could, then sent the message to the infield. Despite knowing our coach had blown a few fuses, he ordered a few boys on the sideline to begin filling the equipment bag, saving himself a few precious minutes at best. But that was all that was needed to set off our coach to his biggest meltdown. He seemed irked more than he was at the umpire moments earlier, shouting across the field with an emotional tirade that was scary. He pointed and shouted and said it was "The most Bush League move he had ever seen." Even though he certainly wasn't the most loving coach on the planet and didn't seem to even like any of us, he didn't like losing at all. He took his position seriously, and believed that winning was more important than teaching or nurturing us. His attitude put us in a strange position. We were there to win and wanted to win, but we were just kids needing coaching and guidance. It was an odd feeling being coached by such a staunch man. He didn't have a son, relative or neighbor on the team, and we'd wondered how he'd come to coach us. Other teams were coached by a father of some player, and as the years went by we discovered that to be the norm. He didn't like other coaches, umpires or even our parents. He didn't like anything, really. He held a chip on his shoulder towards everyone, but despite those shortcomings and flaws, we looked up to him in some strange sort of way. He wanted this game more than others, as if the opposing coach was his enemy. And perhaps he was. Whatever the reason, we sensed it, and because of everything happening, we wanted to win for him.

I recall he said something to Little Jackie that bordered on encouraging. Any words he'd spoken before scared us as if we'd been in trouble. I'd never heard him utter a single word that was meant for building an ego or character, that integral part of coaching young boys eluding him and not seeming to matter. But for some reason, the few words he'd spoken seemed to register with Jackie, and he approached the plate with a purpose none of us had seen from him before. He dug his back sneaker into the box with conviction. He took a few practice cuts with the enthusiasm of a player with confidence. He readied his bat for the first pitch, waving it in the air as if he'd finally figured it all out. And when that first pitch came in, he closed his eyes and swung with all the might he could muster, making contact for the first time in the season.

We were stunned. And as we watched the ball roll ever so slowly towards third, we began jumping up and down for Little Jackie to run, and to run as fast as he could. But this was new territory for him. He was as surprised as we were and the ball slowed to a stop before Jackie took a step. As we implored him to throw down his bat and run, he flung it, striking the umpire in the shin. This delighted our coach beyond words, as if it had been the funniest thing ever. As he roared with delight, the third baseman fielded the ball then slipped and fell on the grass before getting off a throw. Unbelievably, Little Jackie reached base for the first time all year.

As we cheered our lungs out for the little guy, we watched him plant his foot defiantly on the bag with a thud. It hadn't been forgotten that we trailed by five runs, but new life had been breathed into us from the most unlikely of sources. Activity from the boys at the top of our order followed, and as we exalted and made as much noise as we could, there was one problem remaining—one really big problem.

Where Little Jackie was likely to have been the smallest boy in the history of the league, his running speed was the difference in the last play. And with Big Bobby batting next, speed was certainly not a part of his game. We knew this from running drills coach put us through in practice. Bobby not only lagged behind, but he huffed and puffed and collapsed on the ground running from home to home. But he hadn't showcased this lack of speed in any game, and like Little Jackie hadn't made contact with any pitched ball all season. There was no doubting he was the slowest, fattest and least skilled boy in the history of the league. He was more than just pudgy, for he was the most enormous kid to have donned a baseball glove or to have held a bat than any of us had ever seen before. His cheeks looked as if they had been full of chewing tobacco, but nothing foreign was in his mouth. He had rings of fat that climbed clear up his back, and his stomach hung over his belt right down to his knees. Strikeout after strikeout followed him just as often as they had followed Little Jackie, yet, his demeanor continued to be happy. Where Little Jackie was nervous and twitchy, Big Bobby wore a weird smile at all times, even after striking out. And his parents equally jovial and loyal to Bobby and the team as any parents I'd ever heard cheering during any game—despite having no idea what baseball was or about. They'd come from some eastern European country just a few years earlier, and with a last name that contained 14 letters and only three vowels, none of us could pronounce the name or cared to know how. His parents attended all the games, cheering for him like crazy people would. They sat along the sidelines, eating snacks, drinking soda and hoping beyond hope that Bobby would find his way to fit in with the rest of us. They wanted their son to contribute, to fit in somehow to the team.

There were no players left on the bench, and coach rolled his eyes as Bobby went to bat. Coach had a few choice words to say to Bobby as he bounced towards home, and whatever was said seemed to register. Coach removed his baseball cap and ran his fingers through his thinning hair, muttering some form of his unique language we had come to know and understand. But as Bobby approached the plate, something way out of the ordinary happened next. Something very forbidden to the game of baseball.

Bobby was big, but his mother doubled his size. Her rubber arms wobbled and dripped loosely for every arm action, and her wider than life bottom moved from side to side like a bowl full of jelly, even when taking a single stride. I wondered how she had been able to squeeze herself into a car seat, or to walk a few paces without exerting herself. But there she was now, arms bobbing in the air, bouncing and striding towards Bobby and—holy smokes—onto the field of play! Coach seemed overly perturbed as he watched her walk towards Bobby, then he yelled at the top of his lungs to get off the field. She picked up her speed then looked at him with fire in her eyes, telling him in no uncertain terms to "Shush." She moved closer to Bobby, his perpetual smile turning to the most surprised look on a face in the history of surprised faces. She called "Timeout" and the umpire removed his mask, shocked and appalled at what was happening on his field- one he'd now lost any semblance of control over.

She licked her fingers and wiped some dirt from Big Bobby's face, then said in her broken eastern European dialect, "You swing bat today. Swing hard like good boy. Swing like Little Jackie." She wagged her stubby finger in his face and with a dead-serious tone said, "You no make last out today." She tossed back her shoulders like she'd meant it, jiggled and bounced back to her chair before squeezing in and announcing, "Now OK to play ball."

We turned and watched Bobby like a crowd following the flight of the ball in a tennis match. We were speechless and wanted to see his reaction to such sudden and unexpected attention from his mother. He stood in the box and copied Little Jackie, waving his bat in circles. We clapped and shouted with fervor and desperation. A surge of confidence lit up our bench, and our hooting and hollering muffled out those from our opponent. As the first pitch came in our mindset changed from doubt to certainty that we'd pull off the biggest comeback victory of our lives. It didn't take long to keep hope alive.

Like Jackie, Bobby swung a textbook swing, lining a bullet that fell in front of a surprised outfielder. This second miracle in a matter of minutes advanced Little Jackie to second, extending the game, turning over the lineup and having us *believing* that miracles do happen. So much happened in this inning alone; the best feud ever between coach and umpire, a mother stopping the game at its most crucial stage and now this! The God's of baseball seemed to be on our side, and with the top of our order coming up, the chance to bat again seemed within reach. All we needed was the next three getting on base to keep it going, to give me that chance.

David Purdy and Richard Cahill singled to right, sending Little Jackie home, cutting the lead to four and bringing Richard Beebe to the plate. Richard was a star player. Reliable with the bat with baseball smarts far above most kids in the league. But he played second fiddle to me. He was a singles hitter with little power, and seemed to be on base all the time. He hadn't made many outs all season and used his speed and short game to his advantage. But with the bases loaded and the game on the line, he needed to hit one out of the infield. Earlier he'd legged out a few infield hits but the bases had been empty. With force outs possible at every bag, I reminded him of just that. He needed to dunk one in.

The first pitch came in low, sailing through the catcher's legs and towards the metal backstop. Without hesitation, Big Bobby broke home from third, his newfound confidence multiplied for every base touched on his way around the bases. We watched helplessly as he lumbered home, slower than molasses with hardly a chance of getting in safely.

The catcher retrieved the ball and tossed it to the pitcher covering home. Bobby hadn't yet reached the halfway point and was a dead duck. He should have turned back for the safety of third base, but he didn't turn back. Momentum and the burden of weight made it difficult to apply the breaks, and forward seemed to be his only option. The pitcher readied for the pending collision, and as Bobby dropped his head, he stumbled but managed to retain his balance. Bobby snorted like a mad bull preparing to gore a matador, then grunted one final time as contact was made.

It looked as if Bobby had been tagged out as he fell to the ground with an earth-shaking thud. And as the umpire began making the call, the ball rolled out from the glove and away from the play. No call was made. Bobby hadn't touched the plate and the tag hadn't been made. Both coaches began screaming. Dazed and confused, both Bobby and the pitcher tried listening to instructions from their coaches, but it was loud and hectic, and neither boy was at full mental capacity. Bobby needed to roll a few inches to make contact with home plate, the pitcher needed to pick up the ball and tag him out. As the slow-motion of the moment mesmerized us, both boys made their move. Bobby rolled and flopped onto home like a fish out of water—a split second before the tag was made. Big Bobby was safe!

As we circled around him, his mother approached the plate, parting us from her son like Moses parting the Red Sea. She cried tears of joy as she pulled him to his feet, kissing him on the cheeks as if a returning son coming back from years at war. And he didn't seem to mind. He regained his composure for a moment, sporting the biggest smile in the world. He seemed unconcerned that his mother twice had broken an unwritten code of baseball conduct. He was caught up in the moment—his one and only shining and defining moment in baseball. And we felt good for him. It was what he had needed. It was what we had needed.

• • • • •

With two runners on, David Molyneaux was grazed slightly on the shirt from the next pitch. David flashed a knowing look as he took first base then said to me, "Hit it a mile." And with the bases loaded and down by three runs, the game was mine to win—exactly the way things had been destined to happen. As I studied the outfield defense, I'd noticed they'd pulled towards left—just where my four home runs landed earlier. Their nervous coach signaled them to take a few steps back, and when they did, he directed them to step back even further. They'd allow a hit to land in front of them, but there was no way they'd allow the long ball from me to beat them.

None of his strategy mattered to me. I gripped the bat until the sawdust began spilling out from the handle. I positioned the blue batting helmet, then pointed my bat towards centerfield, just like Babe Ruth in the World Series. I understood what this action meant, that I'd look silly and be shamed if something else occurred. But there was no doubt in my mind that it would happen. Too much happened in setting up this scenario, everything needing to happen had happened. I envisioned ending the game with a grand slam, crossing home plate with the winning run. Circumstances and opportunity merged for me again.

I liked the first pitch most times, and the one on its way looked pretty good. I swung and met the ball on the sweet spot of the bat, sending it on a clean and distant flight towards the outfield. This one wasn't down the line or to left-center like the homers earlier, but to straightaway center—the exact spot I'd pointed my bat. The centerfielder turned and ran as fast as he could but the ball went over his head. He retrieved the ball quickly, but with Purdy, Cahill and Beebe running as fast as they could, they scored to tie the game.

I took the turn at second and broke towards third thinking only to keep running. Ignoring a stop sign given by the third base coach, I took the turn wide and headed home. The ball came quickly to the cutoff man, he turned and aimed, and as I headed in, the ball, tag and slide came exactly at the same time.

As my right foot made contact with the plate, it caused my smelly old sneaker to bend at a precarious angle. The plate had recessed several inches below the ground, curling dangerously above the field of play—erosion and poor maintenance the likely causes. For whatever the reason, the top canvas tore away, exposing and ripping the sock underneath. Blood formed and several toes popped out. I could see plainly the big toenail had torn away, but pain hadn't registered yet. As the catcher tumbled towards my foot, the most unusual part of this unusual day happened next.

He began gagging, coughing and making distorted faces caused from the stench emitting from one old and worn out sneaker. In those final seconds of play, he let go of the ball, covered his face, and like Big Bobby earlier, I was safe. The winning run was home.

My teammates sprinted towards home as I lay in agony. Ah, but what ecstasy! I had done it again! Another defining moment, perhaps the most defining! Pain or not, I was the hero, the man in the clutch, the one that everybody wanted to be. Yes, I proved again that I was absolutely, undoubtedly, and categorically the one and only Mickey Mantle, the greatest player in the land!

5

Tommy Behan and The Funny Bone Game

My toe injury did nothing to keep me off the field. There was no question in my mind that it would. Languishing on the bench was lousy, and any concussion, toe injury or future injury wouldn't keep me from playing. Stubborn I would be with that mindset, resiliency added to a growing baseball resume.

I didn't miss a single practice or game as a result of that injury. The big toenail was gone completely, replaced by an underlying ugliness. It throbbed, needed tending to and time to heal properly—up to a year for a new one to grow back fully. Unable to walk normally without limping would take time. Attention and admiration was coming from my baseball colleagues and friends. Baseball injuries suffered from heroic deeds did just that. Limping was purely a reminder to what was done to win that game.

Of course there'd be no need explaining what happened and why I was limping. Stories like this surfaced and travelled far and wide in a hurry around these parts. And as I limped and pretended not to notice the attention, I knew deep down I had become the envy of other players, my injury serving beautifully to broaden my growing reputation. And I wore that injury proudly, a representation of myself and of what I had become.

Injuries connected me to Mickey Mantle onto a higher plain. Mickey learned to play through pain and injury all the time, years of the baseball grind taking its toll on his knees. Unable to perform at peak physical condition must have been frustrating and depressing for him. Yes, I'd been injured and vowed to never miss a single inning, but that was easier said than done. Injuries needed time to heal, and with hardly a day off from the grind, Mickey missed games—lots of them. And if he didn't miss a game, he limped and hobbled his way through one. Prime baseball years were behind him, but I hadn't conceived the thought. I hadn't given much thought that Mickey would retire one day. But his statistics were declining, tumbling in a free-fall along with the rest of the aging Yankees team. I hadn't recognized that, either. The natural spiral of Mickey Mantle's career just hadn't hit me yet, and despite signs all over the place that it was happening, what mattered most was to play through pain and injuries, just like Mickey had. Hobbling and limping through pain we'd manage to do together.

Comparisons between us crossed a new threshold. Batting prowess aside, major injuries reinforced our duo-legend and linkage. My onslaught of tape measure homers over the left field bank at Rec Park continued at a torrid pace. Certainly I was on the verge of breaking the all-time record for homers in a single season, for I was making an outright mockery of the game. Long-standing batting records made by the legends of the game about to be shattered and then surpassed by me. A batting average hovering close to 1.000, the few outs made either screaming liners hit directly at a surprised infielder, or some lucky catch made in the outfield. With eyes like a hawk, I'm certain every swing of the bat resulted in contact with the ball, and that I hadn't swung and missed even once. All this contributed to a status like no other boy held in the entire league, inevitable that all others learned of my reputation as the mightiest of sluggers. It seemed as if nothing could stand in my way.

But there are two sides to the game where greatness is drawn. Where my reputation was earned with raw batting skills and the keenest sense for the game, another boy had been mowing down batters with an incredible fastball. I'd heard about him more and more as the season progressed, but hadn't played his team yet. With games played simultaneously across the three fields, any opportunity to watch him pitch up close hadn't happened. Oh, we'd take a look from time to time, and what we saw wasn't good. His fastball moved scary fast, running past batters as if shot from a cannon. Boys stood far back in the box, shivering and frozen in fear, only a few brave enough to take a swing at nothing but air.

Tommy Behan stood muscled and lean, bordering on six feet tall. From a distance, I'd imagined him as Paul Bunyan, taller and bigger than life, and wondered how a boy so young was cut from stone, imposing as a Greek God.

While we mostly ignored and put Tommy Behan out of mind, the inevitable arrived. Our next game was against his team.

Of course we'd hoped and prayed he'd pitched the maximum innings for the week. Or maybe he'd injured his arm and couldn't throw. Wishful thinking aside, it didn't feel right. Our team had shown no fear all season, although we hadn't faced anyone throwing heat like Tommy Behan, and since he'd faced flamethrowers every day, I wondered how Mickey handled something like this. I decided putting fear aside for the moment to concentrate on accomplishments made so far in the season. And as that concentration and focus took hold, a dead silence fell upon the field.

The usual chatter laced with confidence and security in knowing we were the best team was gone, replaced with a church-like atmosphere and quieter than one on our side. We'd grown used to entering the field like a champion boxer entering the ring, eyes focused on just us. Our swagger and self-assurance was growing and intimidating our opponents, and we'd grown accustomed to a general looseness to pre-game rituals. We'd paired off to warm up our arms, broke down into lines of pepper, and took infield and outfield practice, shagging grounders and fly balls. And through it all, we'd shown little or no attention to our opponent. It was our way of showing strength. Intimidation began long before the first pitch was thrown.

But all the gossip surrounding Tommy Behan changed all that. Talk was, that if he hadn't struck out a player, he'd bean them in the leg or elbow or anywhere else where it would hurt, and hurt for days. We'd heard that a few boys had been hit so hard that they'd quit the game on the spot, vowing to never play baseball again. And the obvious strategy to save one's hide from being beaned by one of his fastballs meant you were a coward, but standing as far away as possible from the plate seemed the most logical and prudent choice in the matter. Striking out was one thing—living to tell about it quite another.

Tommy was but a boy stuck inside the body of a man, with the mind of a boy twice his age. While he knew and understood what he was capable of doing against any batter, facing him squarely in the box was what he'd expected. Courage and honor went hand in hand. Despite the fact his rise to prominence happened as fast as mine, something had to give when we'd face off for the very first time. All the talk and rumors reached a fever pitch.

Rumors circulated that his blazing pitches had hurt his own teammates, that they'd need to change catcher's every few innings just to bring some relief to throbbing catching hands. It was a strange baseball dichotomy. Fear from opponents and teammates prevailed, with his teammates equally afraid of him.

Through all the mind games, thoughts of my 4th grade teacher, Mrs. Paste, came to mind. Mrs. Paste sported a peculiar hairstyle that was matted firmly against her forehead as if pasted on. Frumpy and ordinary looking, her name seemed rather appropriate, living up to its true-meaning. Perhaps names can do that to a person, I thought. I'd used paste in the classroom many times. We'd paint or color any number of award-winning quality drawings, then cut and paste them to the bulletin board for the class to admire. At times like those I wondered and wanted to ask her about this peculiarity of name, but I never did. It would have been considered rude and lead to punishment at home. It was an oddity that stayed with me that entire 4th grade and after.

I didn't know the correct spelling of, *Behan,* or its proper pronunciation. I'd thought his name was *Beaning*, and how appropriate it was. It seemed he had grown into his name—just like Mrs. Paste had, recklessly and willingly beaning defenseless kids with a pitched ball. Tommy *Beaning* was certainly the most fitting name for a pitcher. But Mickey Mantle's name topped them all. People placed trophies and memorable photographs upon one. A place reserved for greatness. At the time I thought fireplace *mantel* was spelled *Mantle*, and like Mrs. Paste and Tommy Behan, Mickey Mantle's name was just as appropriate.

As those thoughts overcame me, the veil of silence continued during pre-game drills. There had been no sign of Tommy Behan just yet. Secretly we'd kept hoping he'd miss the game, that something would prevent him from attending. But as game time approached, our wishes went unanswered. A few kids on the team dropped their gloves, pointing and standing stiff as if they'd just seen a ghost. That's when we saw him emerging from the parking lot. It was Tommy Behan. He grabbed his gear and fixed his cap with a firm rotation. He spit on the ground and stuck a wad of gum into his mouth, filling one side and looking like tobacco. He gave us a cursory glance then made his way towards the field like John Wayne facing a gunslinger. He grabbed a ball from the ground but kept coming, losing not a step with poise and confidence. We may have been scared of him, but he was impressive. I liked what I saw. I liked Tommy Behan.

His manager nodded and handed him a shiny white ball to warm up with, then went down the long line of players. He stopped then pointed at an unlucky boy with his head down, exactly the strategy I'd used in school to avoid being asked a question by the teacher. That brilliant strategy seemed to work most times for me, but this poor kid slumped his shoulders, made simple eye contact with Tommy Behan and put on the catching gear with no sense of urgency.

"What's the matter with you?" Yelled our coach. "Ain't ya' ever seen this boy pitch before?" We froze in our tracks, and the old coach didn't say another word for a while. Instead, he stroked his stringy hair and looked to the sky for some answers. He shook his head a few times as he seemed to do when he was annoyed—which was always—then picked up a bat and held it firmly in his hands.

"Today boys, I want you to use the lightest bat there is, stand back as far as you can in the box, and choke up about six inches." He demonstrated what he'd meant, dramatically standing in the box and choking up as far as I had ever seen any ballplayer choke up on a bat. He tossed down the bat and said, "Don't worry about getting hit, cause' that's when you will get hit." He grabbed one of the plastic blue helmets that bobbled always and fit nary a soul. He poked his fingers through the opening at the ears for no apparent reason, then slid it onto the head of the boy standing next to him. He said knowingly, "And if you get hit anywhere on the body, should be good in a day or two. Don't be babies. Be ballplayers. Now warmup."

Our mouths hung as if there were no supporting bones on our chins. Even I was feeling scared, for the memory of my concussion and toe injury was deep-seeded and so recent. The last thing I wanted was to be gunned-down by a Tommy Behan fastball. *What another motivating speech* from our coach, I thought, as the loudest, *pop*, we ever heard drew our attention to the other team. I looked at the poor catcher shaking his hand vigorously to get back some feeling.

• • • • •

Tommy apologized, impressing me. But what was he to do? He couldn't purposely hold himself back due to his gift. But he seemed very aware of himself and what he was capable of doing with the ball. He'd just apologized to his own teammate—an authentic gesture from the best pitcher around. And I liked that quality in him. I liked it a lot. *We should be teammates*, I thought.

The next pitch came in fast as lightning. The catcher didn't even reach for the ball, but retreated. He was in immediate agony. He shook his hand in obvious pain. Behan took the ball back and said softly, "Get ready, here comes my fastball." What! My fastball! What was the last pitch he had thrown? The catcher stood back a few more feet, squatted and readied himself for the next pitch. Behan began his windup, and as he turned to the right, we locked eyes—and I swear I saw him smile just a little. The pitch sailed in, but my eyes couldn't follow the ball. In the shortest period of time in the annals of league history, the ball transferred from his hand and into the mitt of the catcher, making a sound that caused us to fall back and emit a collective, *Whoa!*

Our coach, Mr. Motivation, took notice. He placed his hands on his narrow hips and said, "I see how it is. A bunch of babies I have for ballplayers." He took the lineup out from his pocket, came over to me and said, "What about you, Mantle? You scared, too?" And then for good measure, "And how's that foot of yours?" His mouth was so close to mine I could tell what his last three meals were. I looked at his wrinkled old, cigarette-smoking face, and could sense the rest of the team looking to me for leadership. I thought back to my plastic army of soldiers, how I had directed them in cases just like this one today. I had been the one to look up to, the one who could bring them out of difficult times, the one and only Supreme Commander. I pulled my head up from the trenches, gritted my teeth, clenched my hands tightly and said, "My foot is good, and I'm not afraid of Tommy Behan." But I was lying.

Our coach stepped back for a few seconds, nodding in affirmation. He said in a way only he was capable of saying, "Good. Then you'll bat first today, and you're pitching, too. Grab a ball and warm-up."

Batting first? Mickey Mantle never bats first! I was cleanup hitter, just like

Mickey was. Bobby Richardson batted first, then Kubek and Maris- that was the order! I looked at my teammates, their eyes reading disbelief in mine. Oh, karma and order was about to go haywire. I pulled myself together, then grabbed a ball to warm-up my arm, all the while thinking about facing Tommy Behan. My first few practice throws sailed wide and high, I couldn't stop thinking about facing him. Would I hit another home run, or—God forbid—strikeout, or even worse—get beaned in the head! Would I be able to see his pitches coming in, would I be able to even swing the bat! Then a brilliant thought hit me. *I'll walk. Just take four pitches out of the strike zone and take a walk.* The thought excited me. I'd be patient at the plate, forgoing hitting homers for the moment to set an example for my young teammates. After all, showing discipline and patience at the plate was needed at times like these. I nodded to myself, completely happy with my decision, for I would save face as the biggest basher in the history of the league, and show that Tommy Behan could be had. They'd write about this day in the annals of league history, meant to be read by for current and future players—something to tell their own kids and grandchildren about.

Behan and his team took the field. He tossed in a few more pitches and the umpire yelled, "Play Ball." I stepped into the batters box and remembered what coach told us earlier. I planted my back foot as far back as I could in the box, choked up about six inches on the bat, and readied myself for the first pitch from this, *Bob Feller.*

Behan looked in. His fearless look likely contrasted with the look of fear on my face. As I took a few cuts and took my batting stance, I noticed the outfielders were pulled far to the right, as if I were a pull-hitting lefty. I knew what that meant. I'd be swinging late. The players on the field started with the usual chatter of, "He's no hitter," and "Come on, Tommy." I gritted my teeth, focused on Behan and wondered why the distance between the mound and the plate seemed off- way off. He appeared much closer and I kept wondering why. He took his windup, delivered the pitch, and before I knew what happened, the ball was back in his glove and the count was strike one.

Strike two came in just as fast. I stepped out of the box and took a look around. Our on-deck hitter looked dazed and confused, and the other players seemed to be in shock at the count. I looked at their puzzled faces and decided it was time to take some serious action.

I'll begin my swing the second he goes to deliver the ball, I thought. I didn't need to actually see the ball. The first two pitches were strikes, and they both seemed to be right down the middle. I pulled myself closer to the plate. The players couldn't believe this defiant move against Behan. I took a few swings then pointed my bat towards center. I inched closer to the plate, dropped my hands down to the handle and made ready. The players from both teams sensed the drama unfolding. The defense took a few steps back, and I glared at the mound towards Behan. The players on the bench began to cheer for me like never before. I was their hero and this was going to be another shining moment in a lifetime full of such moments. Behan took the ball from his glove, took his windup and sent the ball sailing.

I started my swing as his arm came forward, estimating distance and travel time like some scientist. I took a step forward, pulled the bat through the zone, and swung with all the might I could muster. Now, I had never been hit by a pitched ball before, and had never seen a player swing at a ball and get hit by one at the same time, either. The two didn't seem to go together. As my right arm began clearing through the strike zone, the pitch deflected off my right elbow and bounced away. Strike three was called.

Coach argued the call as usual as large tears formed instantly in my eyes. I slumped to the ground and grabbed my elbow. I'd heard adults call it the, "funny bone," but I wasn't laughing at all. It tingled. It vibrated. It hurt more than any prior injury. The pain seemed so different than all the others, another bizarre injury in an injury- riddled season. The assistant coach came over and began rubbing it, and I tried listening to coach arguing while dealing with the pain. He blasted the umpire about the lousy call made and repeated himself dramatically with animated movements and the adult language we'd grown used to hearing. I tried hiding my tears, but they continued to flow. I thought I'd never be able to use that arm again. I couldn't stand it. And as the pain began subsiding, I began thinking about the consequences. I struck out for the first time all year, swinging at a ball hitting me square on the elbow. And I cried on the field like a baby, hadn't hit a homer to centerfield after boldly pointing my bat. They'd have no pity on me. I'd be the laughing stock of the league. No longer would they approach me as a leader or look up to me as a hero. That would all change here and now. No longer would I be the one they wanted to be. My fate had been sealed from this one moment of failure.

Surely I was doomed and about to be outcast.

But something happened to change all of those negative thoughts. As I walked away from home plate, embarrassed and bracing for whatever was to come, the umpire yelled, "Take your base, kid."

"What?"

"Take your base," he said loudly. "You got hit before you swung the bat, therefore, by rule, it's a hit-by-pitch. Good job hanging in kid."

My head lifted regally, I cleared the tears from my eyes. No one had reached base against Tommy Behan, but now, I had. Sure, it hadn't been a tape measure homer, walk or hit, but it was something never before accomplished. I'd be known as the first batter to reach base against Tommy Behan. My legacy would follow as batting champion, home run hero and now, slayer of Tommy Behan. Certainly this would be written in the Hall of Records, used to motivate and inspire others for all time like it was supposed to be, just what destiny had in store for me as the Mickey Mantle of boys.

6

The Girl Named Mickey

Summer hit its midpoint, an incredibly hot and humid one that didn't relent in its promise or purpose. Day after day the mercury read 90 or more, and with a humidity that made us drip beads of sweat and lose our energy, we begged for a break—even for a day or two. But despite the sweltering heat and rising humidity and the longing for a day in the 80's, we were boys. Our needs were simple ones. With an inherent need to explore and to explore some more, any temperature—hot or cold—had no hold on us and couldn't keep us down for long. Although we'd waited for a much-needed break in the weather that didn't come, the decision had been made to explore the surrounding neighborhood just west of ours.

We had gotten up the nerve a few weeks earlier to tackle and cross over into the eastern territory—a decision that left us shaken and afraid—and one we vowed to never tell our parents about. While the fear and anxiety of breaking any border of any neighborhood played on our minds, what we'd heard through the rumor mill piqued our interest. A few older boys living on the fringe of the border had terrorized other brave boys from neighborhoods like ours. Those bullies lived just inside the outlining borders of our two neighborhoods—or so we were told-and word was they didn't take kindly to trespassers, and they'd harassed and even beaten up a few of the unlucky ones. But they were just rumors. We'd never actually spoken to any boy who'd experienced anything even remotely close to what we'd heard. But rumors may just as well have been facts for us, and despite the rumors and the potential consequences, we went in full-steam ahead.

We crisscrossed a few streets at first, weary at all times and on the lookout for trouble. And as we weaved our way up and down each street for several hours, we'd decided it was time for a much needed break. By this point we hadn't encountered any trouble as expected, and in fact, the feeling that was expressed bordered on creepy. We hadn't let our guard down yet, and we hadn't seen another boy, girl, or even an adult—not even a dog, and found that to be somewhat unusual if not outright strange. The neighborhood seemed no different than ours, its houses tightly packed together with just enough space in between. Cars lined the streets from end to end, but lack of activity of any kind really got us to thinking. And as our conversation intensified and we wanted to know what the heck was going on, the first signs of life appeared, and it wasn't good.

Trouble found us as predicted. It wasn't a bully that caused us to start running for the hills, it was a dog—a big, black, mean and ugly dog. We'd spotted him at about the same time he'd spotted us, and while all of us owned dogs, this dog did not appear to be the type to give up his paw or want his belly rubbed. He looked mean and serious. We took off the other way.

Our legs churned and took us as fast as they knew how, with no idea where we were heading. All we knew was to run—and to run fast. I looked back a few times to check on my friends to see exactly where the dog was and how much ground he'd gained on us. I was sure only a few seconds passed, but he'd closed the gap considerably. I prayed for him to stop running. I wished that any adult was watching and would intercede to help us. And just when I'd imagined the sharp fangs of this beast tearing into my flesh, emergency vehicles—a police car and the dog catcher's truck—pulled in right between us and the dog. We kept on running, but we were safe. The dog was cornered and trapped almost immediately.

We stopped running at that point, fresh out of breath and thankful to be alive. The close encounter took me back to the previous winter when I'd been attacked by an entire pack of dogs in front of our apartment. I was about to go outside to play in the snow, bundled up like an Eskimo with layer upon layer of coats, long underwear, mittens, scarf and hat all bogging me down. I recall having been wrapped so tightly I could barely move a muscle, stiff as a popsicle coming out of the freezer. Overboard precautions such as these had been important ones to say the least—catching a cold or the flu or something worse was not an option, and so they wrapped us like mummies. But the cocoon my mother wound me into likely saved my life that day.

At the front door of our apartment they'd met me, almost as if they'd been waiting for me to come outside. I closed the door behind me, but didn't feel any fear from this pack of dogs, and hadn't even wondered where they'd come from or who they'd belonged to. I leaned in to pet one, and he bit me, tearing into the clothing of my coat. I backed off, but others joined in, and before I knew what was really happening, I went to the ground and covered my face instinctively—the only exposed part of my body.

I don't remember how I was saved from the encounter with the dogs, but it changed the way I'd react to dogs. I'd learned a great lesson from that attack, and while I suffered no bite marks to my body, I respected all dogs, continued loving them, but kept a certain distance from them until I sensed it was safe. Our story with the big, black, ugly dog stayed a secret, swearing a pact from boy to boy. But we had decided to set out for the west, still shaken from what could have happened to us had that dog not been captured. And now all the chatter about what could have been ended with what's to be. A certain, cautious confidence was restored, and while I'm sure that none of us really believed it, we assured ourselves that nothing would go wrong this time. We had no idea what awaited for us on the other end, but we were willing to give it a go. We just had to.

. . . . .

We were feeling quite rambunctious, needing some adventure outside of baseball. And the neighborhood to our west had enticed us for the longest time—especially the small line of mountains we could see clearly from the vantage point of the Binghamton Public Library. The mountains seemed fairly close from that point, likely only a few miles at most. We'd plan to leave by nine in the morning, reach the mountains by noon, explore the terrain for several hours, then bust home by three to make it just in time for supper.

So we packed some sandwiches and sodas, gathered our gear and formed a single-file line. Of course I would lead the line, initially traversing the dangerous woods and concrete roads of Recreation Park, then emerging deep from within and onto the other side, ever weary of an ambush from any number of enemies. Certainly we knew what these woods were made of, and none of it was good. Particularly tricky just beyond the carousel, the woods opened up into a denser, darker, more dangerous place to be. Though void of signs warning visitors to beware, these woods were not unlike the haunted forest that Dorothy, Scarecrow, Tin Man and Cowardly Lion pushed through together on their way to an audience with the Great and powerful Oz. Where they successfully battled talking trees, flying monkeys and witches, we'd face even more dangerous critters and monsters- many of them unknown to man. As Supreme Commander, unearthly disruptions and menacing creatures was commonplace. Far and away I held the distinction of being the most experienced and skilled commander the world had ever known. Forging forward with a watchful eye and a keen sense in spotting trouble, any secret held by these woods was no secret to me. Keeping the boys calm was imperative to completing any mission as was remaining unscathed and unharmed throughout the journey. Cool assurance and calmness would be the keys to our success. Designed perfectly for my command, this assignment was certainly not for the weak of heart, or for any mere mortal to lead.

The library stood at the top of a road on the other side of Recreation Park, probably a half-mile or so from our house. I had visited the library often with my mom, checking out any new Hardy Boy adventure books, illustrated Civil War books and others featuring ugly witches and twice as ugly goblins. Escaping into the pages of books went my mind, filtering through and allowing my imagination to take the helm. My evolving fantasy world enlarged and strengthened itself like a growing hurricane, expanding its reach into newer and even more exciting dimensions. I needed no help at all when it came to such things. Every single element of my young life had been wrapped ever so tightly in these burgeoning fantasies concocted at will. With so many tumultuous adventures I'd read about stored within me, I knew beyond the shadow of a doubt that crossing over and out from the edges of the Recreation Park woods, our adventure was just beginning.

Making it safely out from the woods was just our first obstacle to breach. We'd made it hundreds of times before, but now we approached new territory. We crossed Schubert Street and headed up the sidewalk towards the library, passing it as quietly as if we'd been inside. Within minutes we left the safety of what we'd known and conquered, focusing on the mountain range in the distance. But the line of mountains that seemed fairly close when we'd started was further away. And for every step forward, that oddity continued, causing me to wonder if we'd make it all the way—even if we walked all day in trying. Before the thought had any chance to settle, the first obstacle of the day greeted us the second we'd reached the end of the street.

The first street we'd traversed snaked and curved in multiple directions, confusing us as it ended. We had no idea what direction we faced, and while a few of us owned toy compasses that never worked properly, we'd left them at home. Now more than ever it was imperative for us to concentrate and to remember what we'd done and what were about to do. Reversing our direction properly at the end of our journey was vital to any safe return home.

But the adjoining street ran long and straight in both directions. Calmly I asked the boys if any had ever crossed this juncture before, but none had. I glanced down both ends, studying the street for any signs of change. But it seemed to run perfectly straight in both directions for miles on end, away from the mountains we were trying to reach. I thought about Oz again, of how the paved streets of the yellow brick road ran for miles. And while Dorothy made a choice—one that ultimately landed her and her friends in Oz—I had wondered what would have happened had she chosen the other road. Perhaps there'd been (God forbid!) quicksand somewhere down the road, a lake of magnetic-mud that could swallow you whole. And as the thought of quicksand rushed through my mind, I dismissed it, then pushed out my chest and said, "Follow me boys, we advance this way."

I pointed my plastic sword to the left and marched confidently down the street. The boys followed, each looking petrified as we made our way cautiously into another new and forbidden world. There had always been invisible lines drawn at the borders of the neighboring streets, no different than ours at Clarke Street, College Street, Laurel Avenue and Gary Streets. That four block portion of real-estate was our territory, where all the kids I had ever known lived and played and roamed freely at Recreation Park. It was invisible boundaries that other kids on the other streets nearby knew to stay away from, knew not to drift too far into or play anywhere near our turf. Sure, Recreation Park was home for all kids from everywhere around.

· · · · ·

There was an understanding that the ball diamonds and the swing-sets and slides were common ground for everyone from any nearby neighborhood. Breaching the sacred ground of someone else's neighborhood was a different story altogether. There was a certain code of conduct that each neighborhood lived by, and we'd discussed potential consequences in preparation for intruders. Any rules that surrounding neighborhoods established was certainly something we'd thought about before. Rules that we'd all learned to follow had been passed down to neighborhood boys, and we reasoned that they were the same everywhere else. Still, we had no idea what to expect from any situation to occur—and it wasn't likely to be anything good. Of course we'd ignored everything we'd learned. Safety in numbers was our motto that day.

That danger we'd feared the most was detected up ahead—a group of boys playing baseball in the street. I raised my plastic sword signaling the boys to halt. Perhaps 100 or 150 yards ahead from our precarious vantage point we watched them play on. They hadn't noticed us yet, so I raised my plastic binoculars for a better look. I gestured for the boys to crouch down as low as they could, and then placed the plastic lenses of the binoculars against my knowing eyes, rotating the centerpiece for just the right focus. But as I did, I dropped the spyglass suddenly. It slid down my chest and fell to the ground, bouncing against the pavement of the street, breaking into pieces and alerting the gang to our presence.

They stopped playing ball just then, then took a good look at us. After only a few seconds they started walking towards us, at least 10 of them and not looking particularly friendly. They picked up the pace, and with a collective chip on their shoulders, they seemed to be all business. One of them whistled in a series of short bursts, and the shrieking sound seemed to alert others from homes nearby. In short order, their ranks swelled to at least 15 kids. We were in imminent danger.

There was nowhere to hide or to run to—no different than the day the dog chased us before being cornered and detained. But there'd be no police car to help us in this moment of need—that was for sure. And with nowhere to hide or run for safety out of the question, there was nothing left but to take our lumps. Little Jackie asked me who they were, but I didn't know. I nodded as assuredly as I could and told him that "Everything would be alright." I knew I was lying.

While I'd recognized a few of them during the few seconds of peering through the binoculars, I hoped I was wrong. Two of the older looking boys I had seen a few times hanging around Recreation Park with the park's gang – the notorious and feared "Park Rats." And while I had seen them only a couple of times before, it was enough to go by. These two boys may not have been actual members to that gang of animals, but they seemed to be connected to them somehow. The Park Rats were nothing more than a gang of thugs, a collection of misfits and outcasts. The only rule to getting around the park safely was to stay as far away as possible from any and all of them. Avoiding these ratty, rotten souls was imperative to our existence. Park Rats would do whatever they could to make our young lives as miserable as possible. They stole our candy and rubbed our scalps with their knuckles, and with blood seeping from our wounds they'd force us to cry out "Uncle," —the most cowardly word there was. Crying "Uncle" was synonymous with every cowardly word in the history of words, and the Park Rats seemed to thrive on making life miserable for all of us.

As the greatest commander of the collective forces of the world—the one that all others revered and admired like no other in the history of reverence—it was widely known that never once in my storied life had succumbed to crying, *Uncle*. While all others from the entire neighborhood told incredible stories of the Rats and their torture techniques, I'd managed somehow to elude such merciless acts of terror, criminal acts against all that was good in the world. I was admired beyond belief for this alone, and it served as the perfect example to others wondering how I'd been able to avoid the Rats completely.

But just a few days prior to our latest mess, the most infamous clash in the annals of Park Rats history unfolded in front of the clubhouse at the park. The boys and I had just finished another full day of playing baseball, and it was time to go home for supper. As we walked home, I spotted a fresh, five-dollar bill rolling gently across the paved entrance road to the park, a light wind pushing it in the other direction. I said not a word and broke promptly for the bill, tossing my glove and bat behind me. My mind thought about all the candy, comic books and baseball cards that five bucks would buy, and my eyes lit up like a fourth of July display. Sure, I had seen five dollar bills before, but rarely did I own one, even though it had been only a few months since I'd received dozens of fives on the occasion of celebrating my first Holy Communion. While that story has little to do with the telling of this one, suffice it to say I was robbed by another neighborhood loser who'd charged me exactly five dollars in exchange for single shots from his rubber-tipped bow and arrow set. Although he'd extorted my entire wad of fives in record time, his evil ways were short-lived. When my mother caught wind of his scheme and rushed to my aid, she demanded the money be returned in full. And while I'd never witnessed such an incredibly serious side to my mother, she managed to get back all the money and send him away with his tail between his legs.

That story went through my mind as I reached my hand out towards the tumbling bill. But it kept moving away from me just enough each time I'd reach for it. I tried again and again, and then heard the laughter from behind me—an evil laughter we knew well, and it belonged to a bad boy we'd called, Smack.

Evil and loud, his signature laughter sent chills down our collective spines. Although we had attempted on occasion to copy his malevolent laugh—and to do so always in private—none of us succeeded at coming close to duplicating it. Dastardly and evil he was, by far the most despicable person around. He'd had a few run-ins with the law, and dropped out of school. All of us were familiar with his resume, and none of it was any good. He was despised and feared like no other bad boy from the neighborhood, and was known only by the most diabolical name given to a kid in the history of names. Certainly his name was as appropriate as Mrs. Paste's or Tommy Behan's, and *Smack* was the real deal. We just weren't sure if he was called *Smack* because of the harm he inflicted on those unfortunate enough to get in his way, or the unusual smacking sound that came from his mouth after completing each and every one of his grammatically incorrect sentences. Either way, Smack was one bad dude.

I ignored the laughter for the moment. I'd worked hard for that five dollar bill, and no matter who was nearby, Smack, a monster or villain, I'd tuned it out for now. But as I raced and reached for the bill, that eternal and confounding focus that owned me blocked me from hearing the dire shouts of warning coming from my friends. Frantically they tried to warn me that the bill was attached to a string, and that Smack was tugging it every time I reached for it. But I wanted that bill more than anything before in my little life. I wanted to grab it, stuff it into my pocket and claim it as mine. I wanted to run to the little green store that sold baseball cards and comic books, and clean them out of both. But then I heard the voice- the cold, familiar voice of Smack. He said, "Hey kid, you want that five dollar bill?"

I turned to him without thinking of the peril I was in. His posse puffed on cigarettes, chuckling mightily. Then Smack asked the question again- this time with more seriousness and conviction in his voice. I turned to my friends but they couldn't help me. I searched myself and wondered what I could say or do to save my hide. So I did something extreme and completely opposite of anything considered logical. I looked him straight in the eye, declaring boldy, "Yes. I want that five dollar bill."

I fought back tears of fear, wondering how Smack was going to hurt me. And with the unlikeliness that he'd go soft and show signs of respect, I regretted the words that came forth so carelessly from my inexperienced mouth. He'd likely react unfavorably I supposed, choosing instead to have me for his breakfast, and then pummel me for lunch. He'd toss me to the side like a rag-doll and warn me to never tell my parents for as long as eternity or he'd come get me—and do it again for good measure. I'd hoped Smack knew of my exploits, heroism and bravery as I had heard of his dastardly deeds. Perhaps he'd known about my talent on the baseball field and was ready to make a change—that he'd seen the error of his ways, and this five dollar bill was an olive branch attached to a string. It seemed like the right time for him to be more like us, I'd reasoned. Evil deeds and reckless behavior would be a thing of the past. I looked at him confidently, renewed with a new sense of purpose, then repeated loud and firm, "Yes… I want that five dollar bill."

Smack began laughing like a banshee. His shrill and evil pitch echoed throughout the park. He dropped the string and then reached behind him and pulled a Beebe gun from his pants. He took careful aim, pulled the trigger and shot me in the hand.

Not a soul moved from position as I reached for my hand. The pain was dull, not like the pain from Tommy Behan's fastball, the two concussions or the pain in my toe. This pain was different and shocking. It was hard to believe I'd been shot for real—even from the likes of Smack. It took me back to the horseshoe incident, but that was an accident I didn't see coming and this was deliberate and brazen. There was no blood to speak of, only the outer skin was broken. And as I stood in utter disbelief, Smack rushed me, flanked by his lowly gang. He said, "Let me see that hand kid," almost as if he'd cared. I raised my hand and he shouted, "It was just a Beebe gun, let that be a lesson to you and all you other kids, *DON'T MESS WITH ME!*"

Tears formed again as I awaited a real beating. I closed my eyes and clenched my body for the first punch. *Would he go for my gut or for my face*, I'd wondered. I prayed for the intercession of my guardian angel, needing it right now. As I felt him coming nearer, a voice broke the silence, saying softly, "Leave him alone."

I opened my eyes and noticed the familiar face of our neighbor, Jimmy Mack. He was as old as Smack, and for what we knew, was a member of the Park Rats. He rarely spoke to any of us, even though he was technically our neighbor, living just a few houses down and across the street from us. We never knew if he was for or against us or somewhere in the middle, but he never seemed to bother any of us when he was in the vicinity. At one point we'd thought he was the leader of the Rats, several times spotting him in the middle of a Rats gathering. I looked up with a sliver of hope at Jimmy Mack. He looked at Smack, and then looked at me and repeated firmly, "I said to leave these kids alone."

Smack grinned an evil grin and laughed a different laugh than the one earlier. The shrill cry from that evil pitch changed, sounding more defensive and fearful. Jimmy Mack spit at the ground near the feet of Smack, then said, "If I ever see you put a hand on this boy or on any of these other boys, I'll find you and I'll take care of you myself… do I make myself clear?"

Smack would have none of it. Never would he back down from any fight- especially one he'd been challenged to—and this he'd considered a challenge. He gritted his teeth and clenched his fists. He made grunting sounds, animal sounds that seemed to bubble up to the surface like a volcano about to erupt. He lunged at Jimmy Mack, swinging wildly with a right hook that Jimmy avoided like a pro boxer would have. He lost his balance and stumbled forward. He tried to recover, but Jimmy Mack held him at the arm, pinning it behind his back and warning his gang to stay away. Smack squirmed and yelled for help, but Jimmy Mack tightened the grip and pulled on his arm. Smack was in obvious pain. He thrashed and bucked like a fish out of water, doing whatever he could to escape. But Jimmy Mack didn't flinch or waver. His huge muscles flexed as he held and extended his grip even tighter. Exhausted and beaten, Smack relented. He stopped writhing and asked Jimmy to let him go. But Jimmy ignored him and said, "Not until you say Uncle."

It didn't take much time for Smack to comply. He muttered the same profanities we'd been hearing from our baseball coach, and he stood in front of us just as vulnerable as I had been, taking his medicine from our neighbor and savior, Jimmy Mack. Turned out that would be our final encounter with Smack. He never came near us again.

But we were in trouble again, vulnerable and outnumbered in this new neighborhood. I wanted Jimmy Mack to rescue us again, but we'd drifted too far from home. Venturing onto the sacred turf of another neighborhood didn't seem like a good idea anymore. They looked as mean and unforgiving as Smack and his gang. They circled us and eyed us as if we had been specimens inside a cage. Then one of them broke the silence and asked, "What are you all doing over here?"

Little Jackie answered first as usual, pointing to the mountains in the distance and said, "We want to make it to those mountains over there." They all laughed and took a cursory look at the mountains behind them. And then came a few words from an angelic voice, a voice so beautiful and pure. At first I believed my guardian angel answered my pleas, but a girl—a beautiful girl with red hair, freckles and blue eyes—stepped forward and said, "Those mountains are miles from here. At least 10 miles. You'll never make it."

"I think it's more like 20 miles, Mickey," proclaimed a boy to her right.

I was confused to say the least, puzzled that the boy used my name, and wondered why he looked at her instead of me. Even my own boys seemed confused, but after a brief discussion between a few of their members, it was coming clear that this girl's name was Mickey—a weird coincidence for sure. How could it be that two Mickey's from separate neighborhoods met like this? I'd never had a friend named Mickey and never knew anyone who had. It was an unusual name for sure. Mickey Mouse and Mickey Mantle were the only Mickey's I'd ever heard of, and Mickey Mouse wasn't real. I turned to introduce myself, and she responded by placing a baseball cap firmly over her beautiful red hair. Fear went away and was replaced by a tingling inside never before felt. Smitten by her beauty I was, and drawn to her like a magnet. I swear I heard birds chirping above my head and spotted a rainbow form in the sky above us. It was so perfect that a girl named Mickey- the prettiest girl ever- had stumbled into my life.

I recognized her just then as that *boy* hitting home runs almost as regularly as I had at Recreation Park. I'd taken notice to his batting prowess and was duly impressed by his swing and its results But that boy was a girl! I couldn't get that singular notion from my naïve little mind. I stood there in the most vulnerable position wearing the look of young love across my face, wondering how in the world a girl could be named Mickey, and how and why any of this was happening.

But my boys didn't seem to be feeling what I was feeling. I sensed this girl named Mickey was probably going to let us go—or might ask us to stay and play baseball with her and her gang. Certainly she must have noticed my batting heroics on the fields of Recreation Park as I had hers. Visions of standing together in the same outfield came to me just then, the only pair of boy and girl teammates in the history of teams. We'd lead our Yankees to incredible come from behind wins, with her as the girl Mickey Mantle and me as the boy. I was willing to share my name with her, ready to welcome her into my Mantle world. We would go through history breaking records, breaking them again and for good measure- breaking them again. No longer would it be Mickey Mantle and Roger Maris sharing an outfield, that would change to Mickey Mantle and Mickey Mantle—boy and girl sluggers like no others in the vaunted history of the New York Yankees.

She broke the silence and asked me if I was the boy pretending to be Mickey Mantle. Before I could answer the question, she said, "You're name isn't Mickey, mine is." She cocked her head towards her gang and motioned them away. They stepped back a few feet and she said, "Let's see who really should be Mickey Mantle. Your team against ours."

• • • • •

We played ball for several hours on the streets of her neighborhood. We battled it out, inning by inning, proving we were just as good if not better than they were. Although I cannot recall the final score to the game, it didn't matter. We were safe, made new friends, and Mickey seemed to like me as much as I liked her. I watched her move in the field and at bat. I watched her swing like a boy and throw like one, too. But I couldn't keep new thoughts away, thoughts regarding how darn pretty she was, and that she played baseball better than any other boy I'd played with before. I didn't want the day to end. But it did end. Darkness was settling in and it was time to get back home. And as we said our goodbyes, she reached over and kissed me on the cheek.

I thought about that kiss and of her all the way home, giving no thought whatsoever that we hadn't reached the mountains. But in some ways we had. I'd reached a new height for sure, the first kiss of my life so innocently given. I wanted to get down to the fields the next day, first thing in the morning. I'd wait for her to arrive, do my best to convince her to play baseball with me and to be on my team. We'd play together for the rest of that summer- that was for sure. And who knew where things would go.

But as the days and weeks of that summer passed by, the girl named Mickey never returned to the fields, not even once. We never saw her gang again, either, and wondered every day what happened to them. I looked for her every day for the rest of that summer. I wanted to run the bases together, wanted her to join me in the outfield and bat ahead of me in the order. But she never came back, disappearing from my life as if that day never happened.

It was the loneliest of feelings waiting for her, but as the days and weeks moved on and the longing for her to return began dissipating, I stopped looking.

I never saw her again.

7

The Toughest Choice: Batman or Mickey

There had never been any debate in my mind of what I'd meant to the entire world, that my purpose was to protect all that was good and to fight for truth, justice and the American way. There was no question as to what outcomes would follow assignments to save the world from evil empires, then vanquishing them one at a time until all was right.

Despite such responsibility, they'd be placed on hold during the summer months. Taking a break from saving the world needed to be set aside for baseball. Baseball recharged the batteries, enabling me to perform at higher levels in protecting the world. Baseball in the morning, afternoon and evening became our mantra during the three most beautiful months of the year. Saving and rescuing was placed on hold for 90 days as I converted into Mickey Mantle.

As leader of the New York Yankees, I'd lead my men into dens of enemies named Indians or Tigers. It was nothing new since I'd battled Indians at the Little Big Horn and Fort Apache, and taking on tigers routinely during missions within Recreation Park. The time was right to lead the Yankees to first place, finishing strong and victorious in nine of my 10 years. They'd held back the Braves in 58', then battled Pirates, Redlegs and Giants on the final battlefields of October. As my mind struggled with balancing baseball and war, something incredibly exciting entered my life.

The Batman television series hit the airwaves on January 12th of 1966. I loved my Batman comic books, and loved pretending to be Batman almost as much as Mickey Mantle. As Batman, it was my prescribed duty to answer always the Bat Signal appearing suddenly across the skyline of my fair city. It mattered not where I was or what I was doing at the time, it was understood beyond all that was understood that I would abandon immediately the task at hand and depart for Gotham City to finish what others were unable to complete. It was my duty to dial up Commissioner Gordon on the red bat phone in our living room, its plastic covering protecting it from the outside world. I would take the news calmly then assure him in no uncertain terms, that I would figure out the Riddler's dastardly riddles, or decipher the Joker's diabolical jokes. I guaranteed to calculate the Penguin's next move or locate the well-hidden den of the Catwoman. It mattered not, for I had fought them a thousand times before- nay, ten times that number- putting my life in jeopardy once again for my city, country and world.

And here it was, coming to the great screen of television. My mind's eye came to life, revitalized in the form of Batman and Robin. I envisioned the characters coming to life as never before, springing forth like magic from the pages of my Batman comic books and onto the television screen. Life could get no better than this. With the show scheduled to debut in a few months, I read my Batman and Detective comic books a hundred times over and then again until I knew each and every page and caption- just like knowing every pitch from every pitcher in the league.

Advertisements kept us informed and ready for the day. I couldn't wait for the day, feeling as anxious as I'd been for Christmas. I'd envisioned how to prepare for that first episode, and played that milestone day over and over in my mind as if it happened already. I'd be sitting on the green couch in the living room of our apartment with my entire collection of Batman comic books stacked on the floor at my feet. I'd organized them by date, leafing through them at the first sign of commercials. Preparation like this was no different than when we'd pile into our Ford station wagon, head to Johnson Field to watch our local Yankees farm team, the Triplets.

I'd take my entire collection of Yankee baseball cards to the games, shuffling them like a dealer then envisioning Triplets players as Yankees. Lefty Pitcher Mickey Scott was Whitey Ford, Outfielder Tom Shopay was Roger Maris and slugger Tony Solaita became Joe Pepitone. Every Yankee player from my baseball card collection was on that field. No longer was the game played between teams in the New York Penn League, but to teams in the American League—the Yankees against some AL rival. I'd flip through the cards as they took batting practice and grounders until the nine starters were named. And for good measure, Johnson Field became Yankee Stadium. It was that easy to make it happen. It was a switch I controlled completely, a transformation switch that took ordinary into extraordinary in seconds.

But I'd never assigned my Mickey Mantle cards to any player from any Triplets roster. That distinction belonged to me. I'd imagined Mickey bunting every ball easily over the fence in right on this minor league field. Surely the spaciousness that was Yankee Stadium paled in comparison. As I held my Mickey Mantle cards I wondered how far he could hit a ball over the fence, and as that thought took hold and I watched Mickey hit balls landing beyond the parking lot, I knew nothing in the world would outlast my relationship with Mickey. Nothing could replace or compete with him.

But in the ever-changing world of a young boy, likes and preferences changed often. Ambivalence in such matters hadn't distracted me before. I had known for a while that Mickey Mantle was mine for the summer months, and that nothing would compromise our relationship, and nothing else would matter as much to me. With the Batman TV show debuting in the middle of the winter, I had no inkling that a few months from now, those feelings would change.

When the first Batman episode debuted in January of 1966, the days of counting down days evaporated. I became glued to the TV. The first Bat Signal arched across the skyline of Gotham City like a rainbow, its logo encircled like the moon on the brightest night in the history of moons. Bruce Wayne answered the first call from the Bat Phone, his words spoken and heard for the first time. My comic book hero transformed into flesh and blood, no longer just a drawing from a comic book. His words rang true and straight, his handsome features more handsome than imagined. Cartoon Batman came to life.

Batman and Robin fell into the reprehensible trap of the Riddler, lured into his seedy hideout within the rotten underbelly of Gotham City. Their situation was dire. The green-suited villain's high-pitched chuckle was too much for me, his cowardly conduct and disgraceful behavior even more than witnessed in a long and storied career fighting evil. I was caught up in the episode, rooting for Batman and Robin as fervently as I'd rooted for Mickey and the Yankees. I grew upset and agitated at the circumstances, but knew they'd manage to pull themselves out of it. And, Holy cow! They did.

The show ran twice a week from January to April, each episode keeping me glued to the TV as if my life depended upon it. *Nothing* could keep me from watching every episode. Not only was I feeling a magnetic draw to Batman, but found it mandatory to learn from him. I could grow stronger watching him deal with one villain after another, his cunningness teaching me new tricks to help lead my forces. Going forward would be easier with such fine examples of leadership from the greatest superhero of all. The Batman TV series became much more for me than an hour of nerve-racking battles between good and evil. It served as a school, using the examples set by Batman and Robin to emulate them. Invaluable lessons they were. I learned and used every technique they used in battling evil empires of the world, monsters that lurked at the edges of Recreation Park, and of course, the goblins in our closets.

· · · · ·

Baseball season was approaching rapidly, and the cocoon of my mind began its annual transformation into Mickey Mantle. I oiled my glove and played catch with my father and brothers. We took grounders and shagged fly balls. We hit and we ran and slid into bases, preparing ourselves for the upcoming season as usual. I was 10 years old, a year removed from the best season a boy could have. I felt ready to make the jump into the next level as a member of the Binghamton Little League. Surely, my numbers on the fields of Recreation Park served as a prelude for what was to be. As the newest and most exciting member of the Little League, I would hit the longest homers in the history of the game over real fences, single-handedly leading my team to victory, capturing Rookie of the Year and Most Valuable Player awards.

The timing of transforming from Batman into Mickey Mantle couldn't have been more perfectly designed. With the final episode of Batman's first season airing Thursday and Friday during the first week of May, and the baseball tryouts earlier that week, it aligned perfectly as if the whole thing was planned. I would hit tape-measure homers during tryouts, impressing the Little League coaches, enjoying every moment of it before switching to watch the final and most exciting episode of Batman's first season.

Then the rains came on Monday- torrential rains- pushing back the first tryouts by a day. That's when I began to worry. My grand plan had changed by just a day, so it was no big deal yet, but still cause for concern. I'd be able to blast homers on Tuesday and Wednesday, and settle in to watch Batman in the evening. It would be better than I'd thought originally, two of the greatest things about to happen occurring on the same day. To be able to change from Batman into Mickey Mantle on the same day was no different than Bruce Wayne changing into Batman. How perfectly seamless, this transformation of power from one hero to another, as if the whole thing was designed by the Gods of baseball. Ah, life was rich.

The rain that washed away Monday's tryout hadn't let up, continuing into Tuesday and retreating Wednesday morning. I understood what was about to happen. Tryouts would be changed to Wednesday and Thursday nights, forcing me to make a choice unlike any other choice before. It came down to making a difficult choice between heroes. Making a decision was real and immediate. And as the fields dried out, the pull between heroes became a burden too much for even me. I couldn't figure out what to do.

I was distracted at the tryouts on Wednesday night, thinking about Batman more than I was thinking about baseball or Mickey, even more than making a roster spot. My mind was clogged and confused, preoccupied with Batman. That distraction affected my tryout. The long homers that normally exploded off my bat were reduced to popups and grounders, swings and misses and weak foul balls. Throws from the field were off-target, and even my attitude reduced to lackluster at best. No matter how hard I tried, my game was off. I couldn't help myself and what was worse- didn't feel like I wanted to. I went home that evening thinking of Mickey and Batman, understanding that a terribly difficult choice needed to be made the next day.

I tossed and turned that night. I played out the situations, weighing options carefully. I knew I'd have difficulty living with myself by missing Batman. I'd be thinking about it for the rest of my life and couldn't stand the thought. I had stuck with him for the entire season, and watching the final show was imperative, no different than missing opening day to a season. It seemed as unfair as being left on the sidelines after being hit in the head by a bat. No, I *could not miss* the final Batman episode- I *would not miss it* for the world.

On the other hand, I'd prepared myself for two years to tryout. I'd hit the longest homers, thrown with pinpoint accuracy and caught every ball hit at or near me. Certainly coaches would remember what I'd done—hopefully giving me a pass for the absence I was contemplating. There'd be no way to overlook my past, of what I'd meant to the game and potential for the future. My plan was formulated as the final tryout came that Thursday. With a half-hour before Batman was scheduled, I placed my glove on my bat and fastened my baseball cap over my head. As coaches began placing boys into small groups, I went over to my father and told him I didn't feel good, that I had an upset stomach and wanted to go home.

As the great coach of the Sheraton Inn, he looked at me and said it was just "nerves," that I'd get over it. He told me to join the others, but I kept pressing, putting on a sickly face that worked for me in the past, repeating that I couldn't play. I rubbed my stomach, made another face and awaited his response.

"You know what this means?" he asked rhetorically. "You may not make a team if you don't tryout."

"I know," I said. "I really don't feel good."

He paused and looked me in the eye. He stared for a while then said, "Go home and tell your mother."

He turned away and began observing other boys and taking notes. I stood there for a few seconds contemplating what just happened. I thought of Batman and began walking the short distance from the park to home, listening to the chatter of the boys, the sweet sound of ball meeting bat, the clapping and cheering from the sidelines. I stopped in my tracks and turned toward the fields, torn between Mickey and Batman, but Batman pulled harder. He called me with a stronger voice, and I decided to stick to my original decision. I'd abandon Mickey Mantle and baseball just this once, certain that Mickey would understand, even look the other way, and our relationship would remain intact.

I watched Batman that night, but it didn't feel the same. I was distracted during the episode and commercials, thinking of playing Little League baseball, of wearing a real uniform and playing on a real baseball diamond. I thought of my duty to the game and to Mickey Mantle, and felt terribly ashamed. I'd let down the baseball world and Mickey, but especially my father.

I was no hero. I was a deserter and even worse—a liar.

That night I went to sleep and felt as vulnerable as Superman had against kryptonite. I thought about the utter unfairness of the day with no perfect choice to make. I felt dirty and out of place, a coward and a weakling. I apologized to Mickey repeatedly for my actions, crying like a baby. I promised I'd make it up to him on the field of play, that I would show the world what I was made of and that this one slip-up would never happen again. I prayed to sweet Jesus that I'd make the Little League, that any baseball seed I'd planted was enough.

But as Friday came and went, no phone call came. I asked my dad about it and he said solemnly that I didn't make it, that my absence was the difference.

Life as I knew it ended just then. Another year toiling in the Farm League was not an option I'd considered. I had spent two years awaiting the opportunity and blew it with no second chance in sight. I thought everyone knew enough about my exploits on the diamond, and I would be immune to such things. I gambled and lost, overestimating my baseball talent. For the first time in my life, the magic switch I held wasn't working. I'd failed on all levels and wished that I could take it all back.

8

The Dogs of Life

Regaining lost energy and trying to recover from the sudden and surprising results from the tryouts seemed irrelevant. I sulked around the house for days, didn't even pick up a ball or go outside. My comic books did little to help my depression, and looking at baseball cards felt like a waste of time. With no appetite for anything fun, I was lost and alone.

Even being Supreme Commander seemed to have no purpose. Gone was the desire to conquer, and had trouble getting out of bed. Inexperience at such brutal consequences felt impossible to handle. The feeling of utter loneliness from making such a poor decision could never be reversed, and hiding inside myself seemed the only thing to do. Shutting out the world and never playing baseball again would be my sentence. But knowing I was the very best at baseball gnawed at my emotions. I couldn't stand the thought of not playing Little League, couldn't wait for another entire season to show the world my talents. Where life was once perfect and easy, it seemed unfair and hard. How could they not choose me to fill any roster spot of the six-team league? Unfathomable it seemed that I'd have to play another season on the Farm League, to break records again. Waiting another year was an eternity. But I had only myself to blame for this predicament. Batman proved to be the stronger pull, and I wasn't proud of it.

My older brother, John, was the lucky one. He made it onto the Sheraton Inn team, lucky enough to be coached by our father, "The great coach." We pitched more balls to each other in the history of pitched balls and invented new games when there were no other boys around. Even though he was a year and a half older than me, I never imagined we'd be separated by baseball. Envious I was of his position on the team, yet equally proud. Perfectly pressed was his cotton uniform and stirrups. Spikes polished black as coal and cap so clean and professional looking. I wanted to be on that team more than anything, even more than wanting Fort Apache or Johnny Seven OMA. I belonged on that field like no other boy ever belonged on one, and it took everything in me to pull myself together to attend their first game of the season.

But when we pulled into the parking lot of the West End Armory Field for the first time, my eyes took in a most beautiful sight. There were real dugouts and chalk-white baselines perfectly straight from home to first, from home to third, to the cutouts around the coaching boxes and perfect round circles for the on-deck batter. Manicured green grass, as green as green could be, grew neatly around the remaining dirt infield, a raised pitching mound just like the majors. There was a real fence where real home runs could be hit over, bleachers on both sides of the field, a swing-set just beyond the left field fence. West End Armory Field was a miniature sized Yankee Stadium.

I began to see things more clearly, studying the beauty of the field. Much as I'd endure another season on the farm, at least I'd be playing organized baseball. Maybe I'd be called up at some point in the season. Boys did get injured and even a few would quit. Rare occurrences such as these were possible, and I knew I'd have to be next in line for any open roster spot. Those thoughts changed my thinking around. I'd return to the dirt fields of Recreation Park and dig my heels in one more year with purpose and focus like no other player in the history of focus. I'd rewrite all the record books just like the year before, and wish upon a star that some player from some team would move away or even quit. It was a beautiful thought, witnessed firsthand a year earlier when two lucky boys were called up in the middle of the season. I wanted something like that happening, and soon enough I'd be wearing a real uniform, playing on a real baseball diamond, smacking tape-measure homers over a real fence.

• • • • •

I fast-forwarded my magic switch and visualized the crowds at West End Armory Field doubling in size as my legend grew, and doubling again by mid-season. By summer's end, they'd be forced to bring in more bleachers, forced to tear down the fences and bring in police to control the traffic around the ballpark. My team would win every game and they'd write stories about me and interview me for the news. The same coaches overlooking me in the draft would apologize and then resign for such blatant and shameful oversights.

They'd want to get a glimpse of me- Mickey Mantle, playing at West End Armory, far removed from the dirt fields of Recreation Park. They'd pack them in around the dugout like sardines, leaning hard against the fences for a chance at my autograph. They'd scream at me for an autograph, and beg me to pose for a photograph. Of course I would oblige with a coolness that only Mickey Mantle knew. I'd take batting practice and ignore the *oohs* and *aaahs* coming from the stands. I'd walk to the dugout as cool as a cucumber, then throw a signed ball at some lucky kid, giving him hope that one day, he might be the next Mickey Mantle…

But that would all have to wait .The Sheraton Inn was taking the field and my brother John was taking the ball on the mound. He stood straight and tall like he'd been on that mound before, and I felt a deep pride. I took out my deck of New York Yankee cards and looked for the image of Ralph Terry. Like my brother, Ralph Terry was a slim right-handed pitcher, a Yankee through and through. I looked at my brother throwing his first pitch to the first batter, but what I saw was Ralph Terry standing on the mound in Yankee Stadium. He'd mow down opposing batters as usual, just as my brother would now do. He struck out the first batter, then the next, and then the next to strike out the side. He made it look so easy and seamless, poised and professional—exactly like Ralph Terry.

• • • • •

As yet another grand plan played out in my mind, I sat on the bleachers next to the Sheraton Inn dugout, studying the players on the team and assigning each one to a player on the Yankees. I watched in delight as the Sheraton Inn took the early lead and added runs to widen the gap into the 5th inning. It was more than enough time to assign the remaining boys to other Yankees—with the exception of Mickey Mantle. Never would I consider matching anyone to Mickey Mantle, it was sacred ground that only I could cross. I continued the course until completing the task, believing and pretending I was at Yankee Stadium. I rooted for my team wildly, cheering and commenting on every call made. I was the best fan in the history of fans, and knew beyond the shadow of a doubt that my cheering was making a difference, that the team was responding to me, and they knew I belonged with them in the dugout. Despite all that happened, I took the high road and cheered like a fool. Then that all changed in a single moment.

I watched a neighborhood boy approach the bleachers. He was barefoot and tanned with long blonde hair. A few of the pretty girls from our neighborhood were with him. Since he'd shown no interest in baseball, I wondered why he was there. He flashed an odd smile and approached me and my mother, meekly said hello, then began telling us something that shattered my world.

I had never lost a loved one, friend or pet to death before, didn't know the helpless, indescribable feeling that would follow such an abrupt reality. I didn't have a single friend or classmate who had lost one either, so the experience and feeling never crossed uncharted corners of my mind. But when he announced tactlessly that our dog, Spike, had been killed in an accident in front of our house, I was mortified. My fantasy-controlled mind shut down on the spot. As he went on I felt a stinging reality that pricked the bubble of my protected existence, sending me tumbling out into the vulnerable world of reality. As the words he spoke sent a chill down my spine, he continued with the gory details of Spike's death, sending my minds eye directly to the site of the accident. I pulled myself back into my fantasy world just then, knowing that as Supreme Commander I had been in charge to protect those I'd loved. Always I'd been able to change the mighty course of history with words and deeds, achieving victories and conquests with the consistency of a champion. Helpless and broken and with tears in my eyes, I managed to call upon myself to perform the biggest miracle of all. But I knew deep down that earthly abilities and powers had limitations. I wouldn't be able to turn back time and change what happened. I realized I'd be unable to make things as they were, and the loss of Spike was real and final.

I don't recall what my mother did just then. I don't remember what happened in the game. I don't recall the ride home or what my father said after hearing the news. What I do remember was the flood of tears that flowed. Tears that ran deep that could have filled a lake. I cried hard and long and kept on crying. The feeling of loss was numbing, yet so near. I hoped beyond hope that it was just a nightmare, for I loved Spike like a brother. He was a part of the family—that was for sure. But I'd taken him for granted. He would be there always to protect us, to bark away intruders, to warn and shield us, just as I protected the world against evil. Never had I given a thought to losing him and thought he'd live forever, that we'd go through life together as the happiest boy and dog pairing in history.

I loved Spike for what he'd meant to our family. He was our time clock, a friend unleashed from the sanctuary of a fenced-in yard to find us on the ball fields of Recreation Park, to let us know it was time to come home for supper. And now he was gone. I was hopelessly heartbroken.

My heart ached with a pain never before felt. I envisioned his last moments crying at the fence, desperate pleas for help coming too late. I didn't care one iota about baseball, Batman or even Mickey Mantle. I didn't care about bashing home runs or saving the world from its troubles. I didn't care that I hadn't made the Little League or forced to play another season on the dirt fields. I didn't care even if I lived another day, for there was no way I could get through this. What I truly cared about was gone for good...

My life had turned upside down in just a few weeks. I had turned my back on Mickey Mantle, disappointed my father and now my best friend in the world was gone, crying for me in his dying moments. Everything was different and was feeling different. The magic switch that could change everything could change nothing important, and for the second time in days, I felt vulnerable and lost. I would never want another dog again, for there was no better dog than Spike. I would never be able to remove the visions of his last moments, never be able to shake them away. I didn't like life anymore, didn't want to participate in any of it. I wanted the safety and security of my fantasy world, where all heroes came out on top and all was well with the world. I wanted Batman and Mickey and Recreation Park to last forever, wanted the security of a world that was falling apart.

As I cried in my bed, I couldn't stand the thought of facing another day. I wanted to wake up and have my mother tell me that all was well and Spike was outside barking at the neighbors. But I knew that wasn't going to happen. Escaping into my fantasy world could not shield me from any of this. Powers I had relied upon to control everything just ended.

· · · · ·

That horrible evening turned into morning and I was still alive, managing somehow to have made it through nightmares and images of the accident. I stretched and yawned, rays of sunshine broke through the window and the smell of bacon frying filled the room. Everything seemed normal except the sweet yapping from our dog.

We ate a quick breakfast, but I had no appetite. My stomach ached, my head pounded and the bags under my eyes were puffy and swollen. Hardly a word was spoken. But when the dishes were cleared, my father told us to get dressed for a ride in the country. There seemed to be a sense of urgency in his tone, but I wasn't in the mood for a ride. I wanted to stay in my room and think about Spike, to grieve properly for him. A nice ride in the country was usually fun and exciting, but the timing seemed strange. But it was needed, I supposed. Country rides seemed always to free my mind, with rivers, streams, hills and mountains far different than our city life. From such a short distance, the view and perspective felt so fresh and real. We got dressed and hopped in the car.

In my haste I forgot to bring any games or baseball cards. With nothing to keep me occupied, I stared out the window and thought about Spike and wondered where we were going and why. We reached the countryside a while later, but the direction taken by my father was a new one. Picturesque views of the landscape were breathtaking. It helped keep my mind off of Spike for a while. Then we turned slowly down a long, winding dirt road.

We drove a few miles, rocking back and forth against the pebbles and unevenness of the dirt road. I looked to the right and spotted several puppies rollicking in the grass up ahead. My eyes widened as I watched one after the other wagging their little tails and playing with each other. When we approached even closer, I saw a sign that read, *Collie Puppies For Sale*.

Dad parked the car, turned and said to me, "Gary, go pick one out."

I opened the door and took a good look at the puppies. They rushed me, I fell to the ground as they attacked me lovingly, licking my face and nibbling on my clothing. I laughed. All hope that I'd lost felt as if it was returning, I felt alive again, continued to laugh and pet their cute little bodies. They were the most beautiful dogs I had ever seen! Tan, white and black markings throughout, with little tails wagging a mile a minute. As the time went by and the dogs began to pull away, one dog remained, lying on my lap and licking my face.

I stood up and rubbed her head and belly, holding her like a trophy and showing her off to my family. She licked my face again and I cuddled her as close as I could, feeling a similar love I had for Spike. I spoke to her, then for some odd reason, I growled. It scared her and she bolted away. I was upset at what I'd done, and she'd managed to wiggle her little body underneath a sandbox nearby, poking her head out just enough for me to see her frightened face. I realized what I'd done, but I knew- I just knew- that she would be our new dog. I knew that I'd protect her from the growls of the world and that she would protect me. We would go through life together, and she would come get us for supper, just as Spike always had.

I began understanding life just then, how it worked its seasons of life and death and renewal. I realized that my fantasy world was transitioning, that maybe I wasn't any Supreme Commander, Batman or even Mickey Mantle anymore. Death changed that old way of thinking. The clock of the world reset itself in a different way. I'd begun crossing a new bridge and it unsettled me. Never had I felt scared of an enemy, but I was scared now. I was being pulled from both ends of a great tug of war, pulled between fantasy and reality. And I knew there would be no turning back.

Reluctantly, I crossed that bridge with my new dog, Tippy.

9

The Call Ups

There was a raw energy circulating around the park, a fantastic rumor that a Little League player quit his team, leaving an open spot that needed to be filled.

The chatter and rumors were pretty clear. The Sheraton Inn was the team needing a player, and the honor for one, lucky boy would be announced after the games that evening. The boys all dreamed that they might be the lucky one chosen, but they knew of my batting prowess, tape-measure homers and the distinct advantage that the coach was my father. They knew that luck would have nothing at all to do with the outcome. It was a done deal as we took the field for what would be my final game in the Binghamton Farm League.

I hadn't gotten over the fact I wasn't a Little Leaguer, but found the will and transformed into Mickey Mantle again, smashing and bashing helpless baseballs. More power than the year before equaled more homers. Hitting homer after homer seemed easier than before, as did my batting style, running style and throwing style—exactly like those of Mickey Mantle. I overheard the hushed tones coming from the boys as they watched me bat. I'm sure they'd tried emulating me, but with the keen eye of a hawk, strong wrists of a boxer and bulging biceps of an Olympic champion, they just couldn't. I ran with the stride of a sprinter, threw the ball with the accuracy of a Robin Hood and slid into bases with the precision of a Ty Cobb. I caught screaming line drives and dove for ground balls that would have gone by everyone else, ran down the longest fly balls like a gazelle and succeeded effortlessly at every phase of the game. I had built the most impressive baseball resume, and now my time to shine had arrived, time to show the rest of the world what I was made of, and to leave behind a legacy never to be duplicated in the annals of the Binghamton Farm League.

. . . . .

I thought about all of it as I stepped into the batters box for the first time that night. I looked across the field to see if the great coach- my father, and the old coach- Bud Sheehan- were present, but it was far too early. I was sure that by the fifth inning, they'd emerge from the clubhouse adjacent to the field, the great coach holding a perfectly pressed uniform, hat and stirrups ready to be presented to one, lucky boy. I smiled as thoughts raced forward to that moment, the magic switch I so controlled for my entire life working its wonderful magic again. I'd envisioned the boys gathered on the hillside, teammates gathered beside me as the coaches called for quiet. I'd listen intently as they'd begin listing my laundry list of accomplishments, starting and ending with unmatched skill at the plate. They'd mention my keen baseball knowledge and engaging strategy, compare me to John McGraw and Casey Stengel, oh, and at such a tender age! Tears would begin to form in their eyes and they'd try fighting them back but would fail, all the while shaking their heads and admitting how lucky they were to help develop me even more. They'd draw comparisons to the greats of the game; Babe Ruth, Lou Gehrig, Joe DiMaggio, and Mickey Mantle, and would announce that they and others paled in comparison to me.

As the first of my three homers that night disappeared into the sky behind left field, I ran the bases just like Mickey had hundreds of times, looked down at the dirt as I circled past first, for I wanted the memory of that game to stay with me forever, to hold onto the wonderful memories of hitting long home runs on the dirt fields. As I took second base, I thought of the first homer I had hit the previous year, and as I took third and headed home, I thought of the grand slam hit the night my sneaker tore apart. I had earned my way to the next level, and couldn't wait for the game to end. I was ready to accept my new uniform.

I couldn't wait to hold my uniform in front of me, the number, "7" etched in navy blue on the back of the jersey. I'd rehearsed a few lines to say, choosing just the right words to motivate, inspire and direct the boys, just as I had as Supreme Commander. My words would be written in stone, they'd carve a monument in my likeness, list my statistics on a plaque and invite me to inspire, motivate and coach others.

As the innings passed by and another homer flew off of my bat, my mind began thinking of playing games at the West End Armory where real bases, real grass and real dugouts existed. Since first laying eyes on that beautiful field, often I'd thought of homers coming from my bat, landing in the swing-set and jungle gym behind left field, replaced in my mind as Monument Park at Yankee Stadium. I had envisioned all of it before, and now it was right in front of me- all of it! My humble spirit was thanking the Gods of baseball for a second chance to continue on my baseball path and to take the steps I was destined to take.

I came to bat again in the last inning, readying myself for the next pitch. The other games ended, and boys and coaches from those teams began gathering at the far field, waiting for our game to end. Catching just a glimpse of that sparkling blue uniform was on my mind. I smiled a knowing smile as I took another look for the two coaches, and they appeared from behind the clubhouse, making their way over to the far field. I could see the folded uniform in my fathers' arms, the hat and stirrups that rested above. I watched the boys pulling in for a closer look, but the great coach held them back. I smiled slightly before taking the next pitch for another long ride over the left field bank. It was a hit like no other before. It sailed as high and as far as a ball could go, rising and falling like a shooting star, its distance greater than any distance I'd hit before.

· · · · ·

The boys went quiet watching the ball disappear, eyes fixed upon me as I circled the bases for the final time. With another victory secured, it was time to gather my gear and walk over to the far field with Mickey Mantle at my side. I started walking, reviewing everything that was about to happen in my mind. One by one the boys passed me by, nodding with approval and assurance. They ran ahead, excited beyond belief for the pending announcement to be made. Even though I was as anxious as everyone else, I took slow, lasting strides. The importance of what was about to go down wasn't lost on me—but it was also important to be the last boy to leave the fields that night, to take it all in and to remember all of it. As much as I'd wanted to abandon the sandlots for the real thing, there was something inside that was calling me back, something that was slowing me down. I obliged.

I found a vacant spot on the grass along the hill adjacent to the field by the clubhouse. The buzz that started earlier in the week reached its climax. It would all be over in just a few minutes, but I was eager to lean on every word about to be spoken from both coaches about me. I wanted to press the words into the far reaches of my mind where they would be etched forever, pulled out for future use to remind myself of who I was and what I'd meant to the game. I watched as the boys on the grass looked at me as the old coach (and league president) began speaking. But nothing he said was making sense. Puzzled looks on the faces of the others verified what I'd felt, but he kept on speaking, noting accomplishments that were not mine. Perhaps he was confused and mixed me up with another boy, but as he continued speaking and noting more accomplishments, the eyes of the boys turned from me and over to Tommy Behan.

I waited for the old coach to start talking about the long home runs and the accurate throws of mine, of great fielding plays and heroic game-ending hits, but none of it came. Instead, I listened to words about his strong arm and pitching prowess, of strikeout after strikeout, of being the best pitcher ever in the vaunted history of the Binghamton Farm League. I began to sink into the grass along that hillside as Tommy Behan raised his head and smiled wider than I had just moments before. I watched as the boys sitting next to him took notice to the words of the old coach, looking at Tommy Behan with a new reverence that had been reserved for me. My moment of glory was gone.

But as Tommy came forward to accept his Sheraton Inn uniform, I pulled back inside myself exactly as I had the day I'd been overlooked for the draft, and exactly as when Spike was killed. As I retreated away from it all and into the shadows of Recreation Park, I couldn't believe how my life had turned upside down, of how increasingly unfair all of it became with one bad thing leading to another. I was only 10 years old, but everything was changing in the protected world I'd lived in, confusing me and forcing me to think long and hard about everything. Not only had I failed to alter the mighty course of history as Supreme Commander, but my plastic toy soldiers and plastic guns were losing their appeal. The notion that the swing-sets of Recreation Park were means of escaping the enemy, or that the carved horses of the carousel were real horses for the men of my cavalry no longer seemed relevant or real, and it puzzled me. Where I'd faced adversity before, responding to any challenge, my fantasy life was in trouble. And now, as the best player in the history of the game, I had failed again. Maybe I wasn't cut out to play the game at its highest level, or to go down in history as the greatest player there ever was—the greatest player there ever would be. I couldn't even make it to the Little League, to be able show off to the world my God-given abilities as Mickey Mantle.

The road to recovery was once again nearly impossible to handle. Losing out to Tommy Behan was a tough pill to swallow—perhaps the toughest. Yet, I managed once more to return to my roots on the dirt fields of Recreation Park. I couldn't stay away. I couldn't miss a single pitch or an inning from any game. I had bounced back dozens of times before, and I'd promised Mickey I'd never quit. As I held to that promise, I started paying attention more to his leg injuries.

Mickey Mantle was the toughest player in the game. If I continued wanting to be Mickey Mantle, the time seemed right to forge ahead, to face the enemy straight on just like always. There was no room for quitters in the game, for quitters were not allowed in the game of baseball. I would serve more time on the dirt fields swinging for the fences, crafting my game and learning to be patient for my turn. I had gone through a lot that summer, but I would never disappoint Mickey Mantle again, never abandon him again. No, the road to the Little League had not been an easy one, but the road to any single game for Mickey Mantle seemed tougher to me. My father told me that Mickey's legs needed hours of taping before every game and he played in constant pain. Much as my injuries were not as severe or challenging as Mickey's, what I had experienced and what I'd learned about them changed my perspective.

Not only did I need Mickey Mantle, but he needed me. I needed him to continue being the example of what it takes to play baseball, to persevere against anything. And he needed me not giving up on my dream. Our lives were undergoing significant changes—there was no doubting that. I had discovered how vulnerable I was to the curveballs of life, and Mickey showed signs of nearing the end of his career. Yes, I needed to show Mickey Mantle what I was made of, the strength of my character, the perseverance of a champion, the ability to take all that belonged to him and take it forward as him.

The rumor mill started churning its wheel again. Another call-up would be chosen following games that day. We didn't know why, but it didn't matter. Whatever the reason, it came fast without warning or buildup. The boys seemed just as excited as they'd been the day Tommy Behan was promoted, but my reaction to it changed a bit. Disappointment and embarrassment from being overlooked the first time still stung. Hardened as I'd become, I couldn't help having the same expectations and feelings from weeks earlier. I couldn't dismiss the resume I had built. Sure, Tommy Behan was a great pitcher, and we'd learned that pitching was ninety percent of the game, that teams with better pitching won more games than they'd lost. And I'd come to grips with that. Tommy Behan deserved his spot ahead of me.

I had taken a good look at the remaining pitching prospects from our league the day Tommy Behan was promoted. There was nothing special about any of them. Tommy Behan had been the only standout. Since most of us on the Farm League were either nine or 10 years old, arms were still developing their strength, the majority at least a year away from being ready. What Tommy Behan was capable of doing at his age was simply unheard of. I wondered how fast he would be able to throw next year and the year after that. And as I contemplated those thoughts, my attention turned to what I'd contributed to baseball, for what I'd stood for and could be. I believed still that I was the most deserving boy to be promoted, that there was no other boy in the league even close to my talent. I braced myself for the announcement.

We gathered on the same hillside to hear the announcement. But this time, none of us knew which team or coach would appear from the clubhouse. My father hadn't spoken a word about it to me, so I was sure it wasn't going to be the Sheraton Inn again. But as I thought about it some more, a few of the boys caught wind of the boy who'd be leaving. I listened as the name was spoken, and I knew it well. He played on The Sheraton Inn.

At that moment, my father and the old coach opened the doors to the clubhouse and came outside. I prepared for two things—either I'd be accepting a uniform or cheering for someone else. Of course I had prepared a few words to say, but I wasn't going to be embarrassed like I had been a few weeks earlier. Not being chosen a second time by my father was unthinkable.

What I had expected to hear spoken about me two weeks earlier were the words being spoken by the old coach. He spoke of long home runs and a rifle arm that never misfired. He spoke of a baseball IQ well beyond his years, the way he ran the bases and the keen eye at the plate. He spoke of the fairness that comes with baseball decisions, how difficult choices can be. He spoke of Tommy Behan and what he'd meant to his team, of how the decision made that night was most difficult and that it came down to Tommy or me.

My father looked at me and called my name. The feeling of utter jubilation blanketed me from head to toe. I heard the roar of the boys as I accepted my Sheraton Inn uniform. I placed the cap on my head. The tears streaming down my face had come from a different place this time. The clock of the world reset itself in a different way. I struggled with words to say to the boys, utterly lost in the moment. As often as I'd rehearsed what to say, I said nothing. It was as if I'd been in a dream. But it wasn't a dream. It was as real as all else I had faced before. I had made it to the big time. My time had come to show the world what they'd been missing.

I started in right field the next day, nervous and excited. It would be our only game of the season played at Macarthur Field, a nice ballpark but certainly not one I'd been familiar with. Even from afar, I'd felt comfortable at West End Armory Field, allowed onto the field before the games with the team. That familiarity taught me where divots and soft spots were across the diamond, and how to play the corners down the foul lines. I knew where and when the sun would be in the sky, of how to use my glove to shield my eyes against fly balls. Playing at Macarthur wasn't what I'd expected for my first game. And while I was unfamiliar with any of its oddities, I decided not to let it bother me. Mickey Mantle played half his games away from home and didn't seem to have any problems with it. I'd just take my position, do the best I knew how, and do what I could to help our team win.

My first at bat was my most memorable. Facing a pitcher with a fastball rivaling Tommy Behan's, I'd told myself to swing at the first pitch wherever it was thrown, and not to be scared. But I was scared. Butterflies scared. This was big time and I was in it, not on the bench, but as a starter. I needed to impress my new teammates with a hard hit somewhere on that field, hopefully a home run over the fence. I dug my spikes into the box and readied myself for the first pitch. It came in hard and true, heading for the middle of the plate. I swung hard and heard the wonderful sound of ball meeting bat, the ball sailing high and far towards left. I rounded first and headed for second, not knowing if it been caught, landed on the field or over the fence. As I reached second base with a double, the third base coach held up his hands.

I scored my first run a few plays later, advancing to third on a wild pitch and scoring on an infield grounder. As my teammates congratulated me, I learned that my double hit the top of the fence, mere inches from going over. Following the game, I thought about how close I'd come to hitting it out of the park, of how I would have trotted around the bases like Mickey. I had no idea at the time that my long double off the wall would be the closest I'd ever come to hitting a Little League home run. In fact, it was the closest I'd ever come to hitting one in any league thereafter. Ironic it was. The boy destined to break all the home run records would never even hit one. Never.

Author's Note...

The early part of this chapter is based on a letter written to my father on Christmas Day 2006. Forty years passed since that day in 1966 when Tommy Behan was chosen over me. I didn't know it at the time, but the events from that day helped shape my life.

Expressing the notion of unfairness through the eyes of a nine year-old was easy to recapture. Through the eyes and mind of that young boy, the totality of unfairness—or what I thought was unfairness—needed time for the big picture to appear.

Evolution of mind and soul over the next 40 years cleared it up for me. Of course I'd believed at the time how unfair the decision made by my father seemed. Any boy in the same situation would have thought so. As I've had time to think it our clearly, it has occurred to me that the decision my father made that day was not only fair, but extremely difficult. Certainly the level in decisions such as the one my father made was in the name of fairness. We'll never know if other boys sitting on that hillside believed they'd be chosen next, or that they believed they were better than Tommy Behan or better than me. Regardless of that unknown, my father performed his decision at the highest level of decency that day.

I'm sure it was one of the most difficult decisions my father ever made. That decision demonstrated a level of fairness that is rare. No matter how highly I thought of myself as a ballplayer or believing I was Mickey Mantle, the greater need of the team exceeded all of it. Tough love was on display that day. Tommy Behan was the clear choice to make at that time.

Advantages sometimes are often no advantage at all. In fact, nepotism can be detrimental, even destructive. Perhaps the boys on that hillside knew Tommy Behan should have been chosen over me. Perhaps my personal view of my baseball was jaded all along, that I had no business believing I was Mickey Mantle. Maybe I hadn't broken any batting records at all. Maybe I hadn't hit a thousand homers with a thousand more on the way. And maybe if

I had been the one chosen instead of Tommy Behan, it would have caused deeper problems for my father and the team he coached. His decision was made for all the right reasons. Tommy Behan was the right choice.

I have tried living my life in doing the right thing and being fair. I've reached out to loners and outcasts, conscious to not leave one behind. And I'm certain that what happened on that hillside in 1966 has everything to do with it. Drawn I have been to those who seemed lost. Responsibility to be the best beacon of light has been ingrained in me since that day. Although I no longer hit tape-measure homers or run the bases like Mickey Mantle, the further lesson learned from that glorious day is simply to blend the best of qualities from the heroes of your life. The tough fairness of my father... the perseverance of Mickey Mantle...

This is that letter written to my father. It is called, *The Fairest Man:*

To The Great Coach...

Written for my father- John- who gave me the greatest gift of all... 40 years ago...

The 10 year-old boy stood inside the right side of the batters box, planting his right foot as far back as he could along the invisible chalk-line that his imaginative mind had envisioned. He kicked the soft dirt then wiped it smooth with one, clean motion from his tattered sneaker, and adjusted the plastic batting helmet that wobbled precariously against his head. He gripped the wooden bat with his soft, bare hands, and then rotated it until the faded label rested in its proper place.

It mattered little to him which pitch would be the one he would launch beyond the hill in left field. Home Runs just came that easy to him. His thoughts raced ahead to what awaited him following the game, and he smiled a knowing smile, confident and certain that the decision promoting him to the Little League had been finalized. He pointed his bat towards center field like some reincarnation of Babe Ruth, and then took a few swings at the open air. He smiled again as he spotted the great coach- his father- appear beyond the backstop of the second field beyond right field, a clipboard in one hand, and a brand new uniform in the other.

The boy had not yet seen this particular uniform, but he knew it was his. He had watched his older brother many times before this day- this very special day- pull his own gray jersey over his head and tuck the tail neatly into his matching trousers. He had watched him pull the navy blue stirrups as far as he could up each leg, then roll the pants until they were perfectly even from side to side, just below the knees. He had watched him place the navy blue cap onto his head, then slide his feet into the black shoes, their rubber cleats raising his height by nearly an inch. He watched him grab the whitest ball he could find from the ball-bag and place it inside his glove, and he longed for the day when all his brother had would also be his.

The young boy gritted his teeth as the pitch raced towards him. He studied the rotation of the ball, and began uncoiling like some serpent surprising his prey. His perfect swing sent the sepia colored ball sailing into the sky, far over the head of the statue of a boy in left, until it disappeared from view and rolled down the sloping hill behind him. He circled the bases around the rocky infield, and his young mind pictured himself far removed from these conditions of mismatched tee-shirts and trousers, of tarnished baseballs and torn bases, where dugouts were nothing but a patch of ground and baselines were determined by the naked eye of volunteer umpires. But that was all secondary now. It was just a matter of time before he'd be smacking the longest home runs for his new team, The Sheraton Inn.

But, for his young mind, the team wasn't Sheraton Inn and the field they played on wasn't the West End Armory Field. The coach wasn't his father, and his own name certainly wasn't Gary. He would be playing for the New York Yankees, at Yankee Stadium under Manager Ralph Houk, and his name would be Mickey Mantle. Not the next Mickey Mantle, the... Mickey Mantle. He'd be batting cleanup and smashing home runs over the swing-sets and monkey bars beyond the fence in left, pictured in his imaginative mind as the great monuments of Yankee Stadium, where Ruth and Gehrig and DiMaggio were immortalized- and where one day, he would be as well.

The young boys from all the Farm teams began gathering at the base of the green hill where the great coach stood alongside the old coach, Bud Sheehan. There was no doubt they'd been discussing which one of these 50 boys would be the lucky one to be promoted to the big team. The young boy took his place with the others along the hillside, his heart pounding heavily. He composed himself, and began choosing words he would use to accept his promotion to the ringing cheers from the other boys. He wondered how the old coach would review his accomplishments, and how the great coach would introduce him. He sat in perfect confidence as the great coach and the old coach stood shoulder to shoulder, his wide eyes fixated on the perfect uniform nestled in the arms of his father.

The young boy was confused as the old coach spoke of accomplishments that were not his. Perhaps the old coach was confused, for in the young boys eyes he had to be 100. But as he continued speaking, the young boy did not hear the old coach mention his home runs or his skill in the field. Instead, he heard terms like, *great pitcher, great control* and *great fastball.* He grew warm and sweaty and shriveled inside himself, and then looked around for some escape route. He forced himself to look to his left where he could hear the commotion and see the attentive eyes centering on another boy from another team. He shielded himself from any further words the great coach was saying, and pulled himself completely inside himself as the other boy rose to his feet and came forward to receive his uniform.

The other boy seemed as surprised as the young boy had. He held the jersey out for all to see and beamed the widest smile the young boy had ever seen before. The young boy watched the great coach- his father- place his hands around the other boys shoulders, then fasten the navy blue cap of the Sheraton Inn around his head. The other boys stood and gathered around the lucky boy, stroking the raised letters of the new uniform as if it were made of some undiscovered material. The young boy fought back the tears that rolled freely down his cheeks and looked towards the great coach. The great coach squinted and nodded knowingly at the young boy, then smiled and nodded again. But the young boy did not understand what any of that had meant. He picked up his bat and glove and retreated away from the others, brushing back the giant tears that welled up and dropped like huge droplets of rain against the ground.

The other boy had tears in his eyes as well, but they were from a different place altogether. He looked at the great coach and saw him in a far different light than he had before. He had always known the other boy was a better batter than he was, that he could hit home runs with alarming frequency and understood the game like no other boy this age. He knew that he was a good hitter himself, just not as good as the other boy. That was the fact of the matter. But he was a pitcher, and his 10 year-old arm was as good as any boy of 12, perhaps even better. He belonged in the Majors- there was no doubting that. Strikeouts had come that easy to him, and in the one time the two had faced each other earlier in that season, he had hit the boy with one of his fastballs, the one and only time a batter had reached base against him.

Yet, he and the other boys were well aware of the circumstances, and the son of the great coach would certainly be the choice today. He looked in the distance as the other boy- the great coach's son- walked away with his head down and his shoulders slumped…

Forty years later, as the life-changing story grips the young boy who was passed over that day, he thinks of the lucky boy- Tommy Behan- and wonders if what happened on that fateful day in 1966 has affected his life in the same way it has affected his. He wonders if he is fair to everyone as the great coach was that day to him, and if he is sensitive and kind to others- all others. He wonders if that single event so long ago has shaped his life in a way that draws him closer to those who have been passed over, ignored or made fun of. He wonders if that boy has used the decision that was made that day to shape his own life, and if his children have been told the story of that day in the same way he has told it to his two daughters. He wonders if the other boys children are as sensitive and caring as his own daughters have learned to be and wonders if the incredible lesson learned that day has left an indelible mark on his family as it has on his.

As the young boy evolved emotionally and the advance of time has allowed him to understand what truly happened that day, he pictures Yankee Stadium and the great monuments beyond the walls of the outfield, and they remind him again of the West End Armory Field and its swing-sets and monkey-bars. He contemplates the gift his father gave the other boy that day so long ago on that field at Recreation Park, an he knows- he knows- that the great gift given to the other boy by the great coach… was also the greatest gift the great coach had ever given to him…

As a footnote, I'd decided to contact Tommy Behan—and was able to. We spoke at length about that day and what his memories were. He did remember that day, just not quite the way I had. And as we reminisced and talked about our Little League days, I was happy in my decision to reach out to him. Our conversation enabled me to get a good feel for Tommy Behan as a person. I was hoping to hear inflections and tones in his voice that gave clues to character, of someone who cared and remembered. I made the right decision.

10

Eminent Domain and The Little League Draft of 1967

For a few years I had given considerable thought to the really bad things that happen. Sudden surprises like the death of a dog or not being chosen for the Little League to name a few. Fantasy's shield was not much of a factor anymore, dwindling with each and every setback and loss. The old ways of escaping into fantasy and protecting myself from reality had changed drastically, and for good reason. Even though I continued embracing those comforting principles, no longer had I any authority to change outcomes. That string of losses continued its ugly course, visiting us in March of 1967 and calling itself, Eminent Domain.

The cruel winds of change blew into our lives with a fury like no other wind before. Dealing with the loss of Spike was severe and exhausting, the most difficult thing I had ever gone through. But a new dog erased just some of that pain. Death of a pet seemed so unfair. No way to have known what was coming or a chance to say goodbye. But now we faced the death of an entire neighborhood, and there wasn't a thing we could do to stop it.

The old Horace Mann school building needed to be razed. Old age caught up with this beauty. Eighty-seven years of standing had slowed the old gal down. Old wiring, plumbing and heating to name but a few of its problems. Asbestos throughout the building made renovation an unlikely option. Demolition and a rebuild was the answer, resulting in a larger school and parking lot. To make it happen, homes surrounding the school would need to be torn down, and one of them was ours.

"Progress" they'd called it. Considering the circumstances, "progress" was a terribly misconceived word choice. Seven properties would need to go, bought out by the city and their fancy Eminent Domain. And with our house situated smack-dab in the middle of the doomed properties, we'd been told there was no way to fight and win. That would take hiring lawyers, and lawyers were expensive. None of us in our working-class neighborhood could afford to hire a lawyer– even if we'd pooled resources it wouldn't be enough. With the law on its side, we stood no chance at fighting and beating Eminent Domain. What remained was to accept the decision by the city. And so we did.

Not only was our house on College Street standing in the way of their "progress," our old apartment around the corner on Clarke as well. Ironically, the only two places I had ever lived would be among the seven doomed properties. The odds of that seemed so unnatural and punishing. I couldn't believe any of it was happening, that we were being forced to leave the security of our tightly knit neighborhood, the schoolyard and the ball fields and playgrounds of Recreation Park. I couldn't fathom leaving behind the sanctuary that was Recreation Park, and looked upon it as more of a person than a place. Recreation Park was the personality of the neighborhood, of the culture and the fabric that kept us together. It had personality and character. Nothing could ever replace the camaraderie that existed between Recreation Park and us. Nothing.

Six months earlier we'd been handed this sentence from the city of Binghamton. Half a year to find a new home, to say goodbye to our friends and sit back defenseless as the bulldozer did its duty. But while the thought of leaving Recreation Park and my neighborhood scared and upset me, a certain irony played in. Showcasing my baseball game outside of our neighborhood had been on my mind at times, and with no chance at beating city hall, the prudent thing would be to let it take its natural course. Fighting the move was a waste of energy, and energy is what I'd be needing, and lots of it. Pondering and worrying about it anymore was useless. Embracing the move was the practical thing to do.

But my mind played more tricks on me, as usual. Vacillating like I had when choosing Batman over baseball. Life was certainly changing all around us at breakneck speeds and I wasn't sure if I liked it. I had told myself to stop worrying, kept wondering how I'd handle transitioning to a new home and school. And because of Eminent Domain, a part of me was dying. I'd reminded myself repeatedly to relax, but Eminent Domain stayed with me and wouldn't leave. It affected me deeply and it cut to the core. It took away the top layer from our insulated world, stealing the foundation out from under us. It changed my way of thinking. Overwhelming challenges hardened me somewhat, even allowed me to see how the world really worked. And if I'd made it through those, I could do it again.

Along with the changes, I heard the grownups talking often about Mickey Mantle and his decline from stardom. I tried not paying attention to the chatter, but it had everything to do with my hero. They said he was slowing down, that injuries and father time caught up to him and to the Yankees. This wasn't the first time I'd heard it, but I couldn't get used to the idea. Maybe they were right. The Yankees finished last in 1965, then 8th of 10 teams the following year. And Mickey's production dropped considerably. Unthinkable was how I'd felt about it. Since my baseball roots began around 1960, the Yankees had played in the World Series every year, and Mickey Mantle the biggest reason for that stretch of greatness. Looking now at the American League standings and Mickey's statistics in the newspaper was painful. Irony was at work here—and foreshadowing. The rapid decline of the Yankees and Mickey ran concurrent to the decline and fall of our Horace Mann School. With the talk that Mickey was washed up and retirement was imminent, it became apparent that the changing of the guard was set in motion. While I'd understood that all baseball players retired, I hadn't considered this for Mickey. And it played as hard on me as Eminent Domain.

But these changes awakened me and caused me to think. Something extremely exhilarating stirred me, leaving me with mixed feelings of rejuvenation and terror. Perhaps the foretelling of exploring new territories or of conquering new neighborhoods and mashing baseballs had arrived. Perhaps the time had come to put down my toy soldiers and plastic guns for good, to start fresh in a new place, and to pass in and beyond the next open door of my life. I'd felt excited and scared at the same time. Excited for what was up ahead, and scared at what was being left behind. I'd surprised myself by welcoming those pending changes more than I'd rejected them. And after days and weeks of mulling over what the future held, I felt comfortable in leaving it all behind.

None of us watched the wrecking ball take down our house on March 13th of 1967. We loved that house and neighborhood, our neighborhood, *every bit of it*. Although I'd finally welcomed the change of scenery, to see all we'd ever known destroyed in a matter of minutes hadn't interested me. And as the wrecking-ball brought down half our neighborhood, I had no way of knowing Eminent Domain had made just its first stop.

(Our only connection to professional baseball had been minor league games played at Johnson Field, home to the Binghamton Triplets. An aging park not unlike Horace Mann school, the field was located at the epicenter of the expanding highway Route 17—a connector to the New York State Thruway and beyond towards Buffalo. It would be just two short years following the demolition of our neighborhood when the issue of Eminent Domain reared its ugly head once more. This time, Eminent Domain took out an entire baseball franchise—tearing down our beloved ballpark in 1968 for the new highway).

To have experienced two deeply profound demolitions that robbed us of home, neighborhood and baseball team was simply hard to fathom or understand. Everything we'd known involving baseball had been taken. Recreation Park, Horace Mann School and Johnson Field.

In the months prior to the demolition, my parents scouted for a new place to live, checking out houses, neighborhoods and school-systems in and around Binghamton. I'd joined them several times in the great search- but hadn't felt at home with any property. But as our search crossed from Binghamton into the suburbs, one house stood out. Located on a quiet street at the foot of a mountain, we knew this was it. And after negotiations and settlement, we moved into that house located in the town of Vestal.

It was located less than 10 miles from our old house, but it felt like a hundred. There'd be no way to hop on my bike whenever I'd felt like cruising around Recreation Park, or to gather my friends for hours of baseball. Even walking over to the little green store for a pack or two of baseball cards was out of the question. All of it taken for granted, and I missed all of it.

But as time marched on, we adapted to our new surroundings. I welcomed new challenges and the prospect of new friends. Despite the fact I was excited, I was especially anxious and nervous thinking about Little League baseball, playing for a new team in a new city. The question was if I was good enough to make a team.

What I'd heard about the boys of Vestal scared me like nothing else before in baseball. I'd heard how many boys played Vestal baseball, and that every single one was ultra- talented at every position. I'd heard it would take lots of luck for an outsider like me to be selected in the Little League draft of 1967, that being from Binghamton was nothing special. City boys just weren't as good as boys from the suburbs, or so I'd heard. While I had just turned 11 with a half-year of Little League, none of that seemed to matter to the boys of Vestal. I thought I had managed well playing against older boys, but that seemed irrelevant now. The boys of Vestal hadn't thought much of city level baseball, bragging there was no better talent found than in Vestal. And there was no wondering why. I'd been told every sport in Vestal was played at the highest level, with rosters chosen from the very best. There was talk that 700 graduates were in every class from Kindergarten on up, that the high school football team was not only the best in the area, but one of the best in the country, drawing over 12,000 people for every home game. Intimidated was an understatement.

Mind games plagued me before, and this was no exception. Confidence that oozed from me and came naturally seemed to be abandoning me now. Any notion of believing I was the best baseball player around had long vanished. Vestal baseball was superior, that's what I knew. I allowed doubt to creep into the corners of my mind and trick me into believing everything I'd heard, that I had no chance clearing obstacles in the pending tryouts. I had begun to doubt my baseball abilities for the second time in my life, doubted that I had what it would take to make the roster of a new team.

But when winter turned to spring and the great thaw ensued, it was time for tryouts. I was as nervous as I'd been in previous situations, but didn't feel as ready. I oiled my glove and played catch and pepper with my brothers in the driveway, but hadn't taken to a real field yet. I longed for the Recreation Park fields, but they were long gone. Reduced to playing catch in our backyard or on the infrequently travelled street in front of our house hadn't prepared me enough. We'd prospered under the wide-open spaces of Recreation Park, and our narrow street stifled our progress. We couldn't hit a ball, run the bases or throw from any point without keeping an eye out for traffic. Baseball fields of Recreation Park had been taken for granted by all of us. Not having them would likely make a difference.

I thought about that as we drove to the Vestal Junior High fields for the Little League tryout. I was feeling nervous, wanting badly to make an impression. I knew I'd have to hit the ball hard and true, throw the ball accurately and field every ground ball cleanly. I'd need to do all that was necessary to make a team, and hoped that somehow, on a field full of Vestal's finest, I would stand out just enough.

The field was massive, sectioned off into four squares. There seemed to be hundreds of kids, coaches, and parents getting organized around the check-in tables. I swallowed hard as we checked in and was handed a number to pin to my shirt. Butterflies from my stomach reached my throat. I wasn't sure if it was nerves or worry, but I wasn't feeling well. I had shown the first signs of an earache the day before, and was fighting it off as best I could. But my ear was throbbing, feeling as if it was about to erupt, an avalanche of gooey puss working its way forward. I couldn't believe the timing as I pressed my ear against my head, wiggling my earlobe and hoping the pain would subside. But it didn't. It got worse by the minute.

I knew the pain well. My other ear had been lanced in a most rudimentary manner, held down on a table and forced to breath in a substance nearly gagging me before putting me to sleep. But the pain was gone when I awoke. I wanted never to go through it again, but here it was, that same horrible, throbbing pain. It would either take care of itself, or I'd be back on the table screaming for my life. And while time would decide the outcome, there was a baseball tryout to think about and it was just moments away.

• • • • •

I couldn't let this obstacle get in my way, but the pain brought tears to my eyes. As the pain increased, thoughts of abandoning Mickey Mantle for Batman came back to me and of how that decision cost me. I'd vowed to never let anything again come between baseball and me, but pain was doing its best to change my mind. I fought back hard and made my way onto that field, about to find out if I had what it would take. I'd need to muster up something special from deep inside, find a way to manage though the pain and to make Mickey Mantle proud of me.

Other thoughts seemed to be pushing me back to the car, back to the safety of my bed at home. I wondered if it was just a sign to keep me off the field, that my earache was planned to shield me from embarrassment. I was hungrier than all that. I owed it to myself and to Mickey to get out on that field and show the world what I was made of—earache or not. I felt compelled not only to take the field, *but also to take the field*. I could see Mickey and could hear him coaching me along. He was with me all the way, just like before. His strength was taking away my fears, anxiety and some of the pain. I took my hand away from my ear and jogged onto the field.

I gave the pain no thought for the duration of the tryouts. I threw the ball on a dime to every target on the field, and fielded every grounder cleanly without a hitch. I made every play against uneven turf, ran the bases as if I'd owned them and hit every ball clear across the diamond and onto other fields.

Coaches began gathering to watch the next round of batting. The four fields remained active, but I was sure they were coming to watch me bat. For that, I felt at peace with myself, like the Mickey Mantle of Binghamton. I took my turn batting and raised my performance to another level, hitting everything hard and long. With every swing sending balls rolling onto other fields, activity was interrupted. Heads turned from everywhere, players and coaches stopping to watch me bat. Despite an earache that had worsened, I exceeded even my own expectations. I was Mickey Mantle again.

It was thoughts of Mickey helping me fight off the pain, guiding me through another baseball test. He helped me forget past failures and bad decisions, made me look ahead and to believe in all that was to come. When my final swing produced the longest poke of my life, I laid the bat down respectfully, then confidently made my way past the line of coaches .We filled out more paperwork, turned in my badge, and not once did I look over my shoulder to see their reactions. My work was done.

As we made our way home, I knew I was the best on the field that day. I replayed the tryout in my mind, counting the many balls I'd hit that landed on other fields. And as I wondered which team would pick me in the draft, the shooting pain in my ear took over my body. I was in deep agony.

When we arrived home, my father told mom that I "Stood out like no other boy on the field." Endorsement from dad meant everything to me. He was far and away the greatest judge of talent in the history of the game, proving so in the way he'd led his team in practices and games, of how he treated the boys and taught them the right way to play the game. They respected him completely, he'd even made sure to have a case of soda in the trunk of his car for us after every game—win or lose. It meant everything to hear my father say those words.

Until that moment I hadn't considered his feelings about moving from Binghamton. I realized that if he wanted to continue coaching, he'd need to prove himself just as I had to prove myself today. But there were no tryouts for coaches. He was starting over as fresh as I was, facing a distinct disadvantage at being last in line behind others wanting to coach. Long-standing residents of Vestal would surely have the benefit of familiarity. Coaching resume and records would have little merit or value—exactly how I'd felt about the baseball resume I'd been building for years. I was truly sorry for that. My father taught us everything we'd ever need to know about baseball. He spent hour upon hour getting us ready at every level of play. And while my father never tossed his hat into the ring of coaching for the Vestal Little League, I knew down deep what the boys of Vestal would be missing—greatness.

My earache reached a level of pain beyond pain. It pounded, pulsed and brought tears to my eyes. My mother pulled out a heating pad and placed it on her lap, laying my ear gently against its heat. As I lay on her lap waiting for my ear to drain, I waited also for the phone to ring. We'd been promised a phone call later in the day - as long as I'd made a team. I thought to what I had done on the field that day, but doubts started filling my head again. Yes, I had caused coaches to take note of my tape-measure blasts, my accuracy and speed of throwing, my fielding and overall knowledge, but as time went on and the phone stayed silent, I thought maybe they'd been watching other boys and not me, that my uncanny ability to focus overlooked other talented boys around me. I began thinking the worst.

I was shedding tears waiting for the phone to ring and sobbing from the pain in my ear. My mother reassured me I'd be making a team, that coaches were likely mulling over selections and needed time to put it all into place.

Her words were what I'd needed to hear, as if Mickey Mantle was sending a message through my mother. I had to make a team. I did stand out and did show those Vestal boys a thing or two about Binghamton-brand baseball. I wanted that phone to ring more than anything. I needed that phone to ring and I needed it to ring soon.

Within the hour, the phone call finally came. My mother answered the phone and spoke to someone for a few moments. She laughed and nodded constantly, agreeing with everything being said. She thanked him for calling, then handed me the phone. "This is Mr. Bimmler, the coach of the Vestal Police. He'd like to talk with you."

I fumbled for the phone and said hello. I listened intently as Mr. Bimmler told me he'd never seen a better tryout than the one from me. His words were verbatim to what my father said, stating that I'd "Stood out like no other boy on the field that day," and had a "special talent" none of the other coaches had seen in these parts for quite some time. He lauded me, told me that he'd be looking forward to coaching me, and ended by telling me I'd been the very first boy drafted that day—*the very first one.*

Those final words spoken from my new coach lifted my spirits. Not only had I made a team, *I'd been the first pick in the draft*. It was utterly amazing how quickly my earache seemed to heal. I was on cloud nine hearing those words spoken about me. Grand thoughts returned to my mind instantly, imagining myself bashing tape-measure home runs over the left field fence at Angelo Field, and leading my new team to the Vestal Little League championship. I was certain that a young Mickey Mantle experienced the same grand feelings when he'd first joined the Yankees, that he'd made it to the big time after years of hard work and preparation. Adrenalin flowed through my veins. I couldn't wait for the season to start, and I pictured myself standing in the batters box at Angelo Field with the stands full of people watching me bat for the very first time. It would likely take no time at all for the throngs to realize they were watching the face of baseball, and that single-handedly my baseball capabilities would be responsible for putting Vestal on the map.

But in that first year playing in the Vestal Little League, our team of mostly under-12 boys finished dead last—winning but two games and losing 12. I'd shifted from outfield to playing first base most of the season, and despite the failures of our team to win many games, I'd led in most of the batting categories—even made the all-star team. Even with such a dismal season, the final game of the season mattered to our opponent—the Carson's Rotary. They'd need a win to tie for first—and force a one game playoff. Despite the fact my main position was first base, the decision was made that I'd be pitching.

I'd pitched a few games earlier in the season, but hadn't faired well. In fact, a homer I had yielded was voided due to a timeout called by the home plate umpire prior to the pitch. As the unlucky boy circled the bases with the joyous look of hitting a home run over the fence, the umpire raised his arms before he reached second base. He seemed confused and kept running, but the umpire blocked his path. The plate umpire took a moment to explain his call. He'd called timeout before the pitch for some reason, nullifying the pitch and subsequent homer. The homer didn't count.

Certainly I felt relief—but also some pity for the unlucky batter. It wasn't easy to hit a ball over the fence—I'd gone the entire season without hitting one. I had learned that home runs were few and far between in this league— and that connecting for just one might be it for an entire Little League career. Following the unusual circumstances of the moment and sensing the deep despair from the batter, the game went on.

Never before had I witnessed a home run called back due to an umpire's timeout, but what happened next defied the odds entirely. The very next pitch mimicked the previous one—a low, inside fastball at the knees. The batter connected. The ball went high and far and over the left field fence—landing in the *exact spot* as the first one. And there he was, running the bases for the second time on consecutive pitches, elated, relieved and looking as happy as a boy could ever look.

The unfairness that comes often from baseball reversed itself just then. And it was something I'd never see again. Embarrassed as I'd felt at the time, the Gods of baseball showed an unusual fairness that made me feel good inside. It reminded me how important second chances are, of how they rarely work out this way.

That unusual sequence of pitches became a dichotomy of our dismal season. Everything that could go wrong seemed to go very, very wrong. And as I played the season out in my mind and took the mound to face the

Carson's Rotary in that final game of the year, my thoughts turned to the New York Yankees and their sudden fall from grace.

Gone were many of the players from those great Yankee teams from just a few years ago. Roger Maris was a Cardinal, Clete Boyer a Brave, and both Tony Kubek and Bobby Richardson retired. Elston Howard was reduced to part-time play (and would be traded to Boston later in the year), Whitey Ford pitched only part of the season, and the Yankees were no longer battling for supremacy in the American League, fighting instead to stay out of the basement—just like we were.

The old Yankees I'd grown up with had been replaced by the likes of Horace Clarke, Steve Whitaker and Roy White. Even though my allegiance to the Yankees would never waver, it just wasn't the same anymore. Even Mickey Mantle had fallen, and fallen hard. He wasn't putting up Mickey Mantle type numbers anymore. His output of homers was less than half the usual totals. It made me sad and afraid knowing the Yankees were no longer the best team on the planet, and that Mickey Mantle was no longer the best in the game. And while I'd continued likening myself to Mickey Mantle and was sure he and the Yankees would bounce back, it didn't happen. The demise of the Yankees and my last place team reminded me how much we had in common—even in negative ways. But it took some getting used to. The Yankees were one of the worst teams in the league, and so were we.

But I wanted to beat the Carson's Rotary. Last place or not, there was a game to play. With the stands fuller than usual, we took the field. I'd noticed twice as many fans were seated or standing on our side of the field, and it was no wonder. The team holding a slim half-game lead in the standings swelled the stands on our side. Even their parents and coaches were present, rooting for an improbable win from us. It was moments like these I had envisioned so often. I was in the limelight, playing a major role in an all-important game. Despite the fact we'd won just once that entire season, it didn't matter to me. This was an opportunity to shine in front of so many witnesses—reminding me how often I'd been the centerpiece in games played way back in the Binghamton Farm League. An important game like this one hadn't happened to us all year. I looked forward to facing Carson's Rotary fearsome lineup.

They appeared quite confident as we took the field. I'm certain they knew the slaughter was about to begin right here in the first inning, no different than earlier contests between us. They'd had no problems at all with us before, and certainly with their season on the line, it would be no different for this game. But there are lessons to be learned from such arrogance. My sidearm delivery confused them.

• • • • •

They bailed out of the box and took pathetic looking swings. They hit slow grounders and struck out more than they had all season. And as the innings went by and we'd built a slim lead, frustration for Carson's Rotary turned to terror. Victory was within our grasp.

A tantalizing changeup I had learned that year fooled their entire lineup. I'd used it more often as the game went on—especially with two strike counts against the batter. And as their cleanup batter waved at one on the final pitch of the game, the crowd on our side of the field erupted. I don't recall the final score of that game, but it didn't matter. We doubled our win total with the most unlikely win of the entire season, taking down the goliath of the league in the process. While that victory seemed insignificant at the time, it gave us hope for the 1968 season.

Most of us would turn 12 and had been battle-tested and grown stronger. We'd taken our licks but kept fighting trough the adversity. We had an idea we'd be far better than 2-12. And we were. Our Vestal Police team won the Western Division that year. We posted a 12-2 mark—a complete reversal from our two-win season a year earlier. I pitched and played first base, batted cleanup and led our team in batting. And I made another all-star team—just like Mickey always had. All of it felt so good being the very best in the game again. It was what we had worked for and attained—taking our rightful spot where I had always known it to be.

I went through that entire season hitting singles, doubles and triples, but not a single homer. And with the regular season over, I hadn't hit even one during my entire Little League career. Remaining chances for that possibility would in the upcoming championship game against the East Division champs. But we'd be facing John Shanley, their best pitcher. And while my focus would center on performing baseball fundamentals properly, I wanted to hit a home run. I wanted to know what it felt like to round the bases and to be greeted at home—even just once.

· · · · ·

Predictions made to myself were way off the mark. I hadn't become the home run champion of the league, and despite my all-star pedigree, I felt embarrassed by that. Certainly, others believed I'd be a home-run hitter, and likely were surprised at my power shortage as much as I was. I'd played over 40 games over three Little League seasons, probably batted 150 times or more. How was it possible that the greatest slugger the game had ever known hadn't hit a single homer?

I wasn't Mickey Mantle, and was beginning to understand that I never would be. I didn't hit a homer in that championship game and we didn't win the game, either. I ended my Little League season and career with zero home runs. None. How ironic that the closest I'd ever gotten to hitting one over the fence was in my first at bat as a 10 year old, when the ball plunked off the top of the fence, mere inches from going over.

Despite a career with no home runs, other comparisons to Mickey continued. Mickey moved from the outfield to first base for the Yankees, coinciding exactly with my move to first base. Connections were frequent but never noticed by a soul. Always there'd been a way of linking myself to Mickey, as if we'd been one and the same player.

But it didn't matter to me as much as it used to. Where once I truly believed I was Mickey Mantle, I knew better now. I wasn't Mickey Mantle. Although I continued to root for the Yankees, I was thinking less and less of him. I understood I'd fallen way short of being anything like him—and wouldn't become the next Mickey Mantle—that was for sure. It would take a home run hitter for that.

11

The Safety Pin Game

Our 1968 Vestal Little All-Star team set our minds on Williamsport as the United States representative for the Little League World Series- and for good reason. Winning the Vestal Little League Western Division title strengthened our confidence, and with several members from that team chosen as all-stars, we were excited about our prospects. As far as we were concerned, we knew we could go all the way.

As the matchups and playing schedules came out, we had no preferences or dislikes for any opponent. Long before ESPN, and with little scouting reports, advantages were even at best. Newspaper stories was all we could go by. Although we'd read some stories about some standout players, we knew they'd be reading about ours as well.

Already we'd learned the importance of great starting pitching. As potent as any offense might be, pitching was the key. Great pitching could neutralize an entire lineup from top to bottom—and usually did. And while scoring runs in buckets was commonplace during the regular season, these were all-star games, the best of the best. Great pitching could fuel an entire team—and our pitching was excellent. And with each team facing elimination with a single loss, every single pitch and play magnified and mattered to its outcome.

We had no idea we'd need to beat every team in our district, States, and region to secure a spot in Williamsport. What mattered was the next game. Certainly, coaches and parents followed newspaper articles of any team we'd be facing. But they'd kept us away from most of it. The formula was to play our game the way we'd learn to play it. Executing fundamentals of the game by playing flawless defense, moving runners, minimizing walks and coming through in the clutch was the prescription. Precision was the makeup of our infield defense. Dominant was our pitching. Ferocious was our offense. And as I wondered and dreamed of playing and excelling in the Little League

World Series, distant thoughts of Mickey Mantle came to mind. The notion of pretending to be Mickey Mantle had ended—that was true. But long-standing connections came alive in me—especially now when the games mattered most.

Following victory in the World Series, I'd practiced what to say to reporters after being carried off the field and into our winning dugout. I'd laud teammates and coaches, then give praise and credit to the losing pitcher and team before accepting the MVP trophy. Television cameras and microphones would not intimidate me, and reporters would scribble frantically words spoken from me as fast as they could. They'd carry depth and meaning far beyond what would be expected from any 12 year-old boy to say. And when the writers finished their questions and the last bulb flashed, I'd lead the congregation into the dugout of our opponents to pay tribute. My words would be especially deep and meaningful to them, with praise and honor spoken from the heart. The Japanese coach would bow to me, followed by his team. Respectively, I'd ask them to return to Japan with heads held high, to know they'd done their best.

Then we won a few games, and then some more. Confidence and bravado reaching a new level, and we felt invincible. But as each victory was achieved, our opponents seemed to get tougher to beat. We'd whittled away at the brackets, winning one nail-biting game after the other, leaving only the best of the best. Onwards we took our travelling caravan to slay our next opponent.

Hundreds if not thousands of spectators gathered along the sidelines and in the bleachers parallel to both baselines, stretching all the way to the outfield walls. And while our prior games were well attended and full of vocal fans, this crowd was different. Rowdy and noisy supporters of our opponent attracted and distracted us. Clanging cowbells from up and down the third base line was something we'd never seen or heard before, and dozens of hand-made signs of support undulated like a cardboard wave. Such intimidating tactics had not gone unnoticed from our supporters. When we took the field for infield practice, the loudest ovation in the history of ovations greeted us. With our dugout situated on the first base side of the diamond, our fans stayed on their feet, doing their best to cheer above the cowbells and screaming. And as we took our grounders and tried tuning out the noise, we'd realized there was more than one game being played here today.

But we fell behind early. Two more runs in the 3rd put us in a huge hole—and we hadn't yet figured out their pitcher. He was throwing curveballs and sinkers—pitches few of us were familiar with. On top of that was a blazing fastball that was faster than any pitcher from our league, diminishing our chances to get even one batter on base. But in our half of the 4th, the winds of change shifted. Their unhittable pitcher left the mound and took the field at shortstop. He'd reached the limit for innings pitched for the week—a fact we hadn't been aware of until the change was made. We felt renewed as we watched his replacement take his pitches. We sensed we could hit him and hit him hard. His fastball looked liked batting practice speed and he didn't throw a curve or a drop. The rulebook became our friend. We had a chance at catching them and winning the game.

I knocked in our first two runs with a double in the gap then scored two batters later to cut the deficit to two. With two remaining innings, we'd need to hold them, A scoreless fifth from both teams sent the game into its final inning. And as they came to bat in the sixth, something incredibly unusual happened— something on the same level the day Big Bobby's mother took the field.

I took a throw from short on a close play at first, stretching as far as I could. My right leg went straight as an arrow, and my gloved hand stretched as far as it could. The ball smacked into my glove and I felt the runners' foot hit the bag at about the same time. I turned to hear the call, and the umpire dramatically pumped his fist towards the ground, calling the batter out for the final out of the inning. I pulled myself up from the dirt, tossed the ball towards the mound and headed for the dugout. But as I jogged a few steps, I could feel the hot summer breeze against my right leg. I looked down and was horrified! My pants split at the seam from the crotch all the way down to the knee! My leg was exposed to the thousands of unruly fans on the other side. I tried taking myself off the field as fast as I could, and was certain that every spectator, player and coach was watching me. I was embarrassed beyond belief.

I rushed to the dugout and over to our coach. There were no extra uniforms available, no way to patch it up and take the field all mended. I couldn't go back onto the field in such condition. We looked to the boys on the bench to see if any could lend me their pants, but they were much smaller than me. As coach tried figuring out what to do, we looked out and noticed my mother approaching quickly— waving a plastic bag full of safety pins. My mind went back in time again—but not to any game-winning homers saving the day. Instead, my mind went to the only other embarrassing baseball moment I'd been involved in—the day of the infamous smelly-sneaker game.

Never had I witnessed anything like it. An unwritten rule of baseball had been broken that day when Big Bobby's mother came onto our field. It was shocking to most of us, but I was sure Bobby was humiliated. I'd never imagined something so unusual happening to me. Neither incident had a place in baseball. This was serious stuff here. With so much riding on every play in the game, distractions and drama was the last thing needed. My pants were ripped and had blown in the wind like a great sail. I was certain it was hilarious to everyone else, but it wasn't to me. I was mortified. How could I take the field under such circumstances? I'd be an easy target for the boo-birds, and they'd be pointing, laughing and making fun of me. There had to be a way out of this, but there was little time to improvise. And as I watched my mother stride towards our dugout waving that bag of safety-pins, instead what I saw was the image of Big Bobby's mother waving her flabby arms and bouncing in an awkward rhythm as she walked towards him.

"Gary, honey," she said, poking her head around the corner of the dugout. "I have a bag of safety pins, come on out here and I'll pin your pants for you."

Coach nodded, but I froze. My mother violated the rules of the game, and wanted me to leave the sanctuary of the dugout and be exposed to the fans outside. But I had to go. I had no choice. It would be impossible to play the field or bat properly with torn pants, all the while facing the pointing and ridiculing from their nasty fans. So I got the courage up and left the dugout. My mother walked me to an empty chair nearby, but I'd felt so vulnerable and defenseless. One by one my mother began attaching pins to my ripped pant leg. The moment felt even more painful than going to penance at our Catholic church and confessing my sins to the parish priest. This was much worse than that. I was not in a small dark room with a sliding panel and whispering words to the silhouette of a man. I was unprotected and vulnerable to thousands of people, and I knew all eyes were gazing at me and would continue the moment I came out from the dugout.

• • • • •

It became far too much to handle. And as each pin attached, the embarrassment mounted. Not only had my leg been exposed, so had my underwear. Oh, what humiliation!

I had a few minutes to think about things as I sat on that operating chair being pinned by my mother. I was certain Mickey Mantle never split his pants during a game, and if he had, I was sure his mother hadn't rushed down from the stands. As my mother snapped the final pin shut, I stood up to examine her improvised mending job. It was no Picasso. The pins numbered 20 or more, and they weren't the small ones. I'd recognized the pins as ones used on diapers for my younger brother, Doug. With a distinct, pale-yellow plastic top, the silver of the pin glinted against the sunlight. It looked like I was wearing braces for teeth on my pant leg. They were perfectly spaced and stood out like a sore thumb. I ran back to the dugout as fast as I could, the embarrassment hitting a new level.

I tried playing it off like nothing happened, and despite trailing by two runs, my teammates had trouble hiding their smiles. And when we went down in order, I paused at the top step, reluctant to take my position. Coach grabbed my arm. He took a good luck at my mother's handiwork and said, "She did a pretty good job. Better than expected. Don't even think about it. We've got a game to win."

The top of the 6th went our way with my pants put to the test. I fielded a hot grounder headed down the line, then stepped on the bag for the final out of the inning. It was likely the defensive play of game, but more importantly, the safety pins held in place.

I was scheduled sixth in the order in our final at bat, and with a slim chance at best to reach the plate, I thought again about the busted sneaker game and that miraculous final inning. And despite having trouble scoring runs, I believed we'd pull out this game just like that one. I grabbed my favorite bat and waited for good things to happen.

What happened with my pants was a clear sign that this game would finish with a heroic blow from my bat. It was a sign intended for heroes like me to understand. It was no accident my pants ripped open, for without it happening, I wouldn't have given much thought to it. I was being reminded of that game, reminded that everything in our final inning would repeat itself, and would come down to me. We needed two runs to tie, three to win. I played out the scenario in my mind and waited for the rally to ensue.

Mark Mysnyk bunted for a single to start things off, but two strikeouts in succession left us down to our last out of the game. I started to worry. We needed our next two batters to reach base just to give me an opportunity to tie or win the game. Anxiety rose as I watched a fielding error, then a walk. And just like that it happened. The bases were loaded for me, happening in similar fashion to the busted sneaker game.

I strode to the batters box with no thought whatsoever to the safety-pinned pants. Entirely my focus was on the pitcher. I'd doubled off him earlier in the contest—a sharp liner up the gap in left. And he was my type of pitcher. He threw a decent fastball and he didn't nibble. He'd gone straight for the middle of the plate most times, and the middle was where I'd made my living. All that was needed was a well-placed single to tie the game, or a double to win it. A walk would force in a run, but we'd still be trailing by one. And while a walk would pull us closer, a walk is not what baseball heroes are made from. I'd be hitting away.

I could sense the tension in the air from both sides, for I was likely to be the last batter of the game. I stepped out of the box to study the outfield positioning. I gripped the bat hard, turning the handle until I could see the label. The pitcher seemed quite nervous as his first pitch came in high, followed by two more way out of the strike zone. I looked down the line at our third base coach for a sign, hoping he'd have me swinging away. Everyone knew the next pitch was likely to be right down the middle and would be the best one to hit. Everyone knew also that few batters—if any—had been given the green light on a 3-0 count. We'd been taught that a walk was as good as a hit, but that way of thinking was for the weak-minded. And as I hoped for the green light, the "take" sign came instead. I took the next pitch as predicted right down the middle for a strike. The bat rested on my shoulder, and as usual, I took another fat pitch down the middle, running the count full.

I was certain the next pitch would be in the same spot as the previous two. I stepped from the box but didn't bother looking for a sign. This was it. Runners readied to move on contact, fielders readied to make a play. The noise around me was deafening, but I'd tuned it out. And as that final pitch of the game came in, I dropped my hands slightly, stepped forward and swung with all my might.

The crack against my bat produced a beautiful baseball sound. I was sure I'd hit it right where I'd wanted to. The ball rose high and kept on rising. But there was no distance in its course. I'd cut under it slightly, popping it straight up into the air between third and home. And as I watched the ball land inside the glove of the third baseman, I felt sick to my stomach.

The lonely trip back to our dugout was the loneliest I'd ever felt before. Our coaches gathered to tell us how proud they'd been. I had tears in my eyes like never before. I knew that we lost because of me. And like that, our season was over.

I wanted to change the outcome, to put on my hat as Supreme Commander of the armies of the world. But I couldn't take back that last pitch. I couldn't change the flight of the ball to go into the outfield and over their heads, or raise my hands another inch higher before swinging. As badly as I'd wanted to be the hero, I wasn't one. I was the goat.

I wondered how I could pull myself out of this one, wondered how Mickey Mantle reacted at times of failure. It was another difficult time in my young baseball life, and I'd felt like quitting again, to crawl inside my bed and never come out of my room. Baseball had been bitterly unfair to me, but failing inside its flawed beauty made it hard on me. There would be no trip to Williamsport for the Little League World Series, and my final Little League game ended on such a sour note. I had made the final out of the season and let my team and city down, and because of it, I could feel my destiny changing. It confused me terribly. I loved baseball more than anything else, but the game I loved had turned its back on me again. Baseball had betrayed me.

But I was no quitter and needed to get over it. Time interceded and helped heal the wound. I tried putting that game behind me, to move forward to see what baseball had in store for me. I'd certainly tasted the agony and ecstasy that comes with sports- and I couldn't forget that. Quitting baseball was not an option. I couldn't leave the game at such a low point. I'd find a way to rise above it again—just like Mickey Mantle had. And while I certainly tasted the bitterness at failing, it didn't seem right to run away from it. Since success and failure in any baseball game worked in tandem, I'd need to recognize that and get used to it.

But someone had to make the last out of a game. Someone had to make the last play. I'd had my share of ups and downs—that was for sure. Embracing failure was all part of the baseball player package. I needed to remember this and apply it to every aspect of my life. Fairy Tale endings were rare, but I'd keep right on hoping for one.

12

"I Took an Oath."
A Day to Remember: Bus Trip 1969

With baseball ending so horribly bad for me in my final Little League game, I needed some time to get over it—but it wasn't easy to do. I had never failed before in such a critical juncture of a game, able to succeed always in securing a victory for my team. But that all changed now. Making the final out of that game continued reminding me of the consequences in being part of a team, and of how unfair it was sometimes.

Not that life was unfair, because it really wasn't. There was a beginning and an ending to everything. I was just learning to understand how balanced things needed to be. That there was another team on the other side of the field fighting for the same thing we were fighting for started to sink in. That the goals and fears of individuals from those teams had been no different than mine was resonating. That agony and ecstasy prevailed in every at bat and every play in the field was true as well. Lessons learned on the diamond were fast and constant.

Facing the transition from the comforting dimensions of a Little-League diamond and onto a regulation-sized diamond of the Babe Ruth League would be the next obstacle. Home to first was another 30 feet, and the pitching rubber 15 feet back from what we'd grown accustomed to. While the distance from the mound to home offered more time to hit and time a fastball, it was a major adjustment to make. Muscle memory would need to be reset to a new timing. Line-drive hits to the outfield would become routine plays on the infield. And legging out an infield hit or stealing a base seemed unlikely or even impossible. Our arms hadn't developed enough to properly throw a ball from any position with the same result we'd been used to. But there wouldn't be a soul who'd feel any pity for me or any other 13-year-old.

Baseball players adapted. They didn't complain. They'd give the game all they could give and take whatever it gave back.

· · · · ·

As the hibernation of the baseball season began, we turned our attention to football, basketball and bowling. There was a basketball hoop in our driveway; we used the Bennett's field for football and bowled on Saturday mornings in a league at the IBM Country Club. Every day we played some sport alone or together. And as we learned new sports and became just as good at them as we were at baseball, Old Man winter reminded us he was boss of the weather.

That snowy season seemed no different than most winters we'd grown accustomed to. We were as ready for winter as we were for the start of the baseball season. Weather-tested from bitter cold and frequent snowstorms was simply part of the New York culture. Winter conditioned us to be ready—a routine we had learned since the day we'd been born. The annual migration of snow seemed to ignore the calendar quite often. Snow could fall and accumulate in early October and clear into May. Significant snow piled high and deep like some mountain range in Alaska. And when a foot or more fell onto the ground we hoped and prayed that school would be cancelled for the day. But it rarely was. Living in upstate New York called for proactive preparation. Salt trucks and plows roamed the streets. And on rare occasions when school was canceled, we didn't sleep in too long or stay in our pajamas all day. It was a day to make money shoveling snow. We knew just where to go, how long it would take and what we'd likely be paid. Despite the fact the hourly rate varied dramatically from neighbor to neighbor, we had money in our pockets at the end of the day. Enough to buy candy, comic books, and a significant supply of baseball cards.

Our survival skills in handling the onslaught of winter tested us dearly. Winter was long and cold, dark and dreary. But the season would end eventually, giving way to better weather and more outdoor activities. Of course we longed for summer when we could ride bikes and play ball all day. Being stuck inside for weeks and months took its toll, our pent-up energy ready to burst. Staying indoors for hours on end just didn't cut it. Sure we'd go sledding and ice-skating, but there was really no competition in that. We needed to play some game or sport outdoors, bad weather beside the point. And while football was our game of choice during the fall season, we discovered a new sport to play, and it was street hockey.

We had learned to play street hockey the year before, improvising as we had with baseball. Four metal garbage cans angled precisely against a stonewall represented goal posts. And unlike access to dozens of boys when we'd lived in Binghamton, only a few boys joined in to play, mainly our next-door neighbor, Mark Gajzik. And we improvised. We'd invented and altered so many games it became the natural thing to do. There was never a problem inventing or adjusting to a new set of rules. If we lacked proper equipment, we used our imaginations. If just a few boys made up a team, we adapted and made it work.

We'd followed hockey and pro basketball for the first time the previous year. With the baseball season behind us, we'd discovered a new set of players to cheer for. Willis Reed and Walt Frazier of the Knicks. Brad Park and Vic Hatfield of the Rangers. With Marv Albert announcing both Knicks and Rangers games on radio, we fell in love with his voice and with our new teams. I'd tried imitating his voice and the way he called a "goal" in hockey games, using static sounds from walkie-talkies to mimic the crowd noise. We followed new heroes all the way to the end. And as we transitioned our love and affection to new teams and new players, the transition continued for our beloved Yankees, and for Mickey Mantle in particular.

The Yankees had been losing, and losing big. Since their World Series loss just a few years ago against the Cardinals, they had placed no higher than 7th in following seasons. And they hit rock bottom in 1966, finishing dead last in the 10 team American League. It was certainly something to behold, something not accustomed to seeing or even believing would happen. The Yankees had been American League champs every year of my baseball life, and in the World Series five straight years. It was an inevitable changing of the guard, but as we kept up hope that the tide would change, it didn't. The Yankees kept on losing.

It was hard to fathom, and especially hard to see what was happening to Mickey. I couldn't accept his sudden and dramatic slide from the pinnacle of baseball to being on a last place team. He hit only 64 homers in those three Yankee losing seasons following the 64' Series, and batted just .261. And he'd missed 112 games, frequent injuries and leg pain forcing a move from the outfield to first base. His numbers continued trending down, only 18 homers and an embarrassing .237 batting average, the lowest of his career.

Playing the same position as Mickey was the one common thread remaining- just enough to keep our connection alive. Game winning home runs and winning teams seemed to be a thing of the past for both of us, my Little League team finishing in last place and so had the Yankees—hardly the connection one would aspire for.

Then sometime in that winter of 68', our father announced that he'd won a trip for two to Yankee Stadium, a bus trip won from a random drawing at JC Penney's Department Store. Of course we were excited beyond belief. The chance to see Mickey Mantle and Yankee Stadium was actually happening. But as our excitement died down, we'd realized only two tickets had been won. The math wasn't adding up. Two of us would have to stay home.

My heart pounded more than a heart was allowed to pound. It beat against my chest faster and harder than ever before in the history of heartbeats. I thought of all the reasons my father should choose me as the lucky boy, and it made perfect sense to me that Id' be the natural selection. My older brother had been to Yankee Stadium a year earlier with his friend, and I cried myself to sleep when he left without me. My younger brother hadn't paid his dues. He was only eight years old and just learning about baseball and the Yankees. He hadn't travelled the same rocky road that I had, and wasn't yet a strong follower of the Yankees. In fact, I knew more about the Yankees and cared more about them than my brothers had combined. And everyone knew my feelings about Mickey Mantle. In my mind, it was an easy decision to make.

These were sound aspects of reasoning, perfect points had it been a court of law. And when my father explained why he'd chosen me, I didn't need to defend myself. He reiterated the sound reasons I had prepared, his words spoken as if reading my mind. I didn't need to say a single word. Our father made it very clear that I would be joining him on the trip, that I was the bigger Yankee fan, and that it was my turn to see the Yankees. Doug would get his chance one day. I was going to Yankee Stadium.

On top of it all, the tickets were for the Old-Timers' Day game! A two-inning affair played prior to the regular matchup between the Yankees and the Oakland A's. What a coupe! Not only would I see Mickey Mantle, but other greats I'd read about. Joe DiMaggio, Phil Rizzuto and others! I would be seeing the newest home run king of baseball, Oakland's Reggie Jackson, and take in all of the sounds and sites of Yankee Stadium. More importantly, I'd be seeing Mickey Mantle, live and in person for the very first time.

I circled August 9th on the calendar, then began the countdown. I was beyond excited, couldn't contain myself. I would finally see my hero in the flesh, probably watch him slug a long home run into the upper deck. I'd watch him circle the bases in person—even for just this once. Only 260 days separated me from watching Mickey Mantle and the New York Yankees. But as the days elapsed and dragged, I was caught off guard. In a short and unrehearsed conference, Mickey Mantle announced his retirement from baseball.

I couldn't believe it. How incredibly unfair and cruel it seemed. I'd spent most of my life waiting to see Mickey Mantle, a moment sealed by destiny bringing two champions together for the very first time, stolen away from me like so many other things before. I was reminded again about the laws of baseball and of life itself. Of the balance that is necessary for change to occur. I had recovered from heartbreak and disappointment many times, rebounding like a champion. But it still wasn't fair. That Mickey had said he could no longer hit the ball as he had in his prime could have waited one more year. But he was hurting and hobbling all the time. It was time to go and nothing would change his mind. He was done with baseball.

I lost my way for several days after the announcement. I was so upset that I would never see Mickey Mantle play for even one at bat. I couldn't live properly with that thought. I thought back and wondered why we had never gone to Yankee Stadium before, but no matter what I'd thought, none of it mattered. The days long passed when I ruled the world as Supreme Commander and controlled every single aspect and result. It was over. I felt empty.

Despite the dire news, I continued counting down the days, trying to put the painful thought of Mickey retiring out of my mind. I would make the most of the trip, and I would move forward just as Mickey would have wanted. I began entertaining the notion that Mickey would rescind his retirement. I allowed my imagination to take over as usual, envisioning the Yankees trailing by a run in the last inning with two outs and a runner on base.

. . . . .

Suddenly, a fast-moving rumor spread throughout the stands. The first wave of fans who'd noticed something peculiar started pointing towards the Yankees dugout, then row by row, more fans rose to their feet. A player hobbled to the bat rack, dragged himself out of the dugout and public address announcer Bob Sheppard would announce, "Now batting…number seven…Mickey… Mantle."

The standing ovation lasted forever, exactly as I'd imagined it. Mickey would tip his cap, ignoring the deafening noise from 50,000. When the ovation subsided, he'd take a few left-handed cuts inside the box, ready to get down to the business at hand. With the entire audience standing as one, the count would run full, barely fouling off a few pitches just to stay alive.

Hope ran throughout the stadium, but it was different this time. It wasn't the same hope that played the Yankee Stadium stage for 18 years, nearly two decades of clutch performance under pressure. Mickey limped back onto that field to win one more game with a long home run. With fingers crossed and prayers sent, we waited.

The home run he would hit on the very next pitch would sail high and far, higher and farther than any ball ever been hit before in the history of the game. We'd watch the ball take flight, the sound so sweet and so wonderful to the senses. Where it would ultimately land would be insignificant. It would reach its peak, then drop like a shooting star beyond the upper-deck and clear out of Yankee Stadium. Mickey would take the bases for the final time, head down as he always had done before. He'd be greeted by the entire team at home, and then disappear inside the dugout, leaving the game on his terms.

With the fantasy ending, my father told me Mickey was invited to play in the Old-Timers' game and had accepted. This was good news. I felt renewed, as if it had come together from my latest thought. Maybe the superhero-like powers of my youth hadn't totally abandoned me yet, that abilities to change things for the good were possible still. Whatever the reasons were, the gods of baseball were shining down upon me with a golden beam of light. His appearance in the game wouldn't be the same as a regulation game, but it would be something. I was grateful for that. Sure, I wouldn't see Mickey Mantle at his best, and understood this exhibition game was more for show than tell. It was only two innings, meant for showcasing the greats of the game and to restore great memories they'd provided. It would be a game for memories—that was all. That would have to do. I would see Mickey Mantle-just once. I'd be able to tell everyone I'd seen my hero at the plate.

As I continued counting the days down, my first year of Babe Ruth began, and the transition was tough. The base paths were longer and the walls to the outfield seemed 500 feet away from home. Everything seemed much bigger than I'd expected and thought I was ready for. But I wasn't the only one facing the daunting task of getting used to such dimensions. An entire crop of 13 year-olds was with me. But as we practiced and learned to adjust, the season took its course and new distances began feeling normal. By mid-season we'd grown totally used to the fields, and by seasons end we could hardly remember or believe we'd ever played on a Little League field. Our arms and legs got stronger, our bodies were changing, and the better players emerged and showed how adjustments were made.

When the season ended I was chosen as a 13 year-old all-star along with nearly the same boys from our Little League all-stars a year earlier. That excited us. We were familiar with one another, and had something to prove. I certainly did. Memories of making the final out of that final game stayed in the back of my mind. Perhaps I'd have the chance to redeem myself at some point in an upcoming game. I felt ready and willing to face anything—even batting in the final inning with the game on the line. I had tasted both ends of baseball agony and ecstasy, keeping them close enough and far enough apart in my heart. But they were too close to separate. Any baseball player had experienced both ends before. It was natural. Only one team could win any game, and personal highs and lows ran its course for an entire game. I wasn't the only one who'd failed before. Certainly, others on that team recalled some play could have gone our way—something that could have changed its outcome. But I had learned not to be so hard on myself, but wasn't easy to grasp. I replayed that final at bat a thousand times, wishing for another chance—just one more chance to change what happened. But all the wishing in the world wasn't going to change anything. What was needed instead was circumstance and opportunity. I wished for that as the games began.

We won a few games, advancing to play Elmira. Where our games were close, Elmira was winning big. But home field was ours, our Chevron Field playing host for the day. But as I focused on what I needed to do to help advance us to the next game, I looked at the upcoming schedule and my heart sank like a lead weight.

A win against Elmira would move us to the next game scheduled the very day of our trip to Yankee Stadium. I asked my father what would happen if we'd won, and he simply told me I had to play, the team counted on me, and my responsibility didn't end until the final out was made. It was that same tough love demonstrated when he'd selected Tommy Behan over me for the Little League. And I wasn't surprised at that. He said that if we'd won against Elmira, he'd take one of my brothers with him to Yankee Stadium or give the tickets away. It was as simple as that.

I kept my feelings inside, but I was in a deep funk. He must not have understood my connection to Mickey Mantle, that there'd be no way I'd miss the trip of a lifetime I'd been counting down to for over 250 days. I didn't care if our team won or lost. In fact, I began hoping we'd lose that game.

But as such horrible thoughts pounded inside of me, I understood everything about being a ballplayer, the sacrifices made by heroes. And as I contemplated these negative thoughts that made me feel ashamed of myself, more sensible thoughts returned. I couldn't let my team down again—not two years in a row. And as much as I wanted and needed to see Mickey Mantle, I couldn't let him down, either. The memories of abandoning Mickey for Batman returned with a vengeance just then. I shook my head and gritted my teeth. But the other thoughts kept coming back. I couldn't miss going to Yankee Stadium to see my hero. I wanted to beg my father for understanding, to explain what I was going though and how unfair it all was. I couldn't believe it was happening again.

I had no part in any decision. I would play against Elmira, and would miss the trip if we'd won. Action needed to be taken, and fast. Perhaps I could fake an illness or come up with an injury to take myself out of the lineup. My acting at such times worked for me always, so they'd be certain to fall for my act at least one more time. I had missed church several times in the past with such an act, even missed school a few times for no reason at all, other than the upset stomach I pretended to have. I wasn't sure what to do.

On the other hand, I could stay in the lineup and make a costly error on purpose, or strikeout at a key spot in the game. But I needed to make it look real—and that would be difficult. Never had I intentionally missed a ball swinging or fielding—and never knew anyone who had. In fact, I'd always gone all out for any ball hit in my vicinity, and always tried hitting the ball hard somewhere. And now I was asking myself to deliberately commit an error or strikeout. The quandary I was in was unbelievable.

I decided to show up for that game. Mind games plagued me the night before, going round and round with every scenario I could think of. I thought of every possible way for our chances at winning to be reduced, of how I could sneakily make something happen with one or two botched plays in the field. My mind was racing with ideas as we pulled into the field and began warming up. As I looked around at my fellow ballplayers, I couldn't get any of it out of my mind. They had no idea what I was going through here, having no idea what I had endured over all these seasons to get me to this point.

I took my usual position at first, but my desire and attitude changed. While constantly thinking about making errors in the field, or striking out on purpose, the image of Mickey Mantle kept appearing in front of me for every negative thought. I understood expectations and the natural thing to do, and throwing the game wasn't one of them. I believed that Mickey truly understood my dilemma, and how difficult this decision was. I envisioned him coaxing me onto the field, whispering, "Do the right thing." And I wanted to do the right thing, but wasn't sure I had it in me anymore. I was likely the most confused boy in the history of confused boys. Something had to give.

•   •   •   •   •

I hated the feeling feeding inside me. I was a husk and felt guilty. I had been stripped of everything I thought I'd stood for and left standing behind a great lie. The integrity of my young life that had been defined by heroic deeds and monumental home runs was on the line. The guilt and shame haunted me, and now my soul was in jeopardy. No one would ever know if making an error or striking out would be deliberate. It would be a deep, dark secret that I would take to my grave, lasting memories likely haunting me for all eternity. It was getting to be too much to handle.

Elmira scored first and took a 2-0 lead into the 4th, and a part of me was feeling satisfied, almost relieved. Maybe Elmira would add to their lead and I'd be in the clear. Perhaps none of my dark secrets would come to fruition, and we'd lose the game without incident. But it wasn't so. We put a man on with two outs, a double putting him in scoring position, and I was up.

I had hoped for this opportunity all along, hoped for an opportunity to change the outcome of the game. And here it was. *Unbelievable*, I thought. And as the pitcher took his windup and sent a fastball sailing towards the middle of the plate, I lined a shot into the gap in left, knocking in our first run of the game. I stood on 2nd base brushing myself off, with mixed feelings of both guilt and pride still weighing on me. But in that moment, I had grown from a boy to a man with one swing of the bat, defeating the demons plaguing me for several days. Mickey Mantle was undoubtedly with me, guiding me and protecting me from myself. And while emotions coming from moments like those aroused me for a while, I still harbored mixed emotions. I wanted to go to Yankee Stadium. I wanted our team to win. My double hadn't changed those feelings, only enhanced them.

• • • • •

We changed our defensive alignment next inning. Our regular right fielder was injured and they put me in his place. Right field was my natural position most of the year so making the switch didn't bother me. I'd made routine plays and the hard ones all year, and knew every flaw and soft spot across the entire outfield. If I were to botch a close play in the outfield, it would come as a big surprise to those who'd been watching me all year. That we still trailed in the game eased self-inflicted conflict inside, but the enormous guilt was a heavy burden and was killing me. I couldn't be the one responsible for a loss—it had to come naturally.

Their first two batters reached base, bringing up the heart of their order. Their next batter clubbed the ball hard all day, responsible for their runs from an earlier double. He was a real good hitter, able to take the ball where it was pitched—his earlier double down the line in left contrasting with his triple down the right field line in the first inning. I reminded our centerfielder of this, telling him to be ready to go either way and to go hard. The next swing left his bat in a hurry and headed for the gap between right and center. I raced with all my might for the ball, tracking it as it took off like a rocket. I remember racing as hard as I could, my glove outstretched as the ball began its descent. And as I gave chase and thought this was the absolute perfect time to let the ball fall in, another random thought came to me out of the blue. It was *The Little League Creed*.

Continuing my path to the ball, the words, *"I will play fair and strive to win, but win or lose, I will always do my best"* came to me. Like a warning or reminder, I was hearing words recited before every Little League game. The Creed meant something to me, reciting each word precisely and with conviction. Bad thoughts circled back, playing tricks with my mind. The result from the upcoming play could go either way—that was for sure. Not a soul would ever know the truth if I simply let the ball fall beyond my outstretched glove. I wouldn't be blamed for trying to make a great play that didn't work out. They'd tell me it was a good try, that I gave it my best shot, and that I did all I could. They'd tell me I had a good jump on the ball, that it was a clean double, and not to be hard on myself. And as those thoughts crossed my mind, I picked up the pace, kept my eye on the ball, then reached out my glove as far as I could.

Half the ball was sticking out from the webbing of the glove, but I'd made the catch. I got my footing and threw back to the infield, doubling the runner off first, saving two runs, keeping the game close and saving myself from myself.

We lost the game, 4-1, ending our season. But, I'd done my best and overcame negative thoughts that played upon my psyche. For that I am grateful to this day. I had faced my past and moved forward with my life. I heeded Mickey Mantle's advice, to the Little League Creed, and from the gut instincts inside. We lost the game—but I had proven again to myself and to

Mickey that I was *really* cut out for this. Those horrible inner-thoughts of trying to lose the game deliberately had been our dark secret—thoughts that no one else on earth ever needed to know about. But the gods of baseball watched me closely. I'd earned the privilege to see Mickey Mantle play baseball, and did it the right way.

Following the loss to Elmira, I was drained emotionally. All the ins and outs thinking about what to do in that game zapped my energy. But I'd made it through. Despite losing that game, I repelled all the negative thoughts plaguing me, feeling clean and whole again. I had cleaned my conscious and saved my soul with the decisions made during that game. I knew what was at stake. The old memories of abandoning Mickey for Batman just wouldn't go away, and they never would. I'm certain that if we had lost that game because of some selfish decision, I'd never be right again. I'm positive of that to this day.

Nothing stood in the way to see my Yankees and Mickey Mantle. I checked off the last of the 250 days from the calendar then packed a few things for the bus trip to New York. I said goodbye to my mom and brothers, and headed for the pickup location with my father.

First and foremost I packed my glove for it was really the only item I would need. To catch a ball was rare, but having a glove increased the odds. Foul balls could be tricky, coming from all angles and speeds, even caroming off raised hands and objects. Even though I'd never come close to catching one at any Triplets game, I'd noted this peculiarity. And while there'd be 50,000 others at the same game, it didn't matter and never would. Catching a foul ball required considerable luck, and having a glove was the safe and easy choice.

We boarded and left on time. It would take about four hours to reach the Bronx. Enough time had been calculated to settle into our seats at least an hour before the Old-Timers' game. I'd attended just one other pro game a couple of years earlier, and remembered the long lines for hot dogs, souvenirs and even for going to the bathroom. But that crowd at Shea Stadium was under 17,000—a third of the expected crowd for the Yankees game. Because of that, I wanted to get into the stadium as soon as possible, get what we needed and settle into our seats to watch batting practice, perhaps even catching a glimpse of Mickey Mantle.

As much as I had been in awe of Shea Stadium, it was Yankee Stadium I'd longed to see, learning enough of Yankees history in the past two years, and Mets history was dismal and still developing. Drawn I was to everything Yankee Stadium stood for. The giant structure, the Monument Park in center, the pennants and World Series flags blowing in the breeze. It was a building suited for winners.

Our bus travelled down Route 17 making good time, smooth and steady as she goes. I talked baseball with my father, told him just a little bit about my feelings about the game against Elmira, but not enough for him to know the secrets I'd harbor for decades. I studied the batting statistics of the Yankees in the Sunday paper, the standings of both leagues, all the while sitting on pins and needles and feeling anxious. And just when I was feeling pretty good about making good time, the traffic pattern changed.

Motorists were blasting their horns at one another, some weaving in and out from lane to lane and cutting ahead of others. Traffic slowed to a crawl then stopped completely. I was a nervous wreck without the traffic problem, and without a single vehicle moving an inch, it wasn't looking good—we were going to be late. Within just a few minutes, traffic started moving at the posted speed limit. Whatever problems there were seemed to have ended, and I was grateful for that.

We came within a few miles of the Bronx when our driver slowed down again. About a mile back we'd passed an abandoned car on the shoulder of the road, all four tires missing and sitting awkwardly on makeshift blocks. He muttered something as he took a good look, then pulled the bus over to the side of the road, placed it in park, and walked outside.

We watched him light up a cigarette and run his free hand through his hair, all the while pacing up and down the road. He was talking to himself and seemed agitated beyond belief. I asked my father what was wrong and he said he didn't know. He left his seat with a few other men and went outside to find out. From my vantage point I could sense something was terribly wrong. He was annoyed and fidgety, speaking incoherently, waving his hands and pointing towards the city. The men didn't seem amused with his antics, even threatening him to get back in the bus and start driving. He flicked his cigarette, returned to his seat and called dispatch.

My father told the rest of us on the bus what was happening. Apparently this was his first trip driving to the city, and from what he'd heard he was scared to go any further. That we'd just passed a shell of a car, well, that didn't help matters much. He remained fidgety and incoherent, stood up and admitted it had been a bad idea right from the start and that he couldn't continue driving. We'd have to wait for a replacement driver to take his place.

I couldn't believe it. The Old-Timers' game was less than 90 minutes from starting, and looking at miles of traffic inching by didn't exactly leave me with a warm and fuzzy feeling. Although I had no idea how close we were to the stadium, hope seemed lost. I wondered why it seemed so hard to see Mickey Mantle just one time.

Other boys on the bus seemed equally upset as I was, but I was certain they hadn't been as vested in Mickey as much as me. None of them experienced anything like the path I'd taken to reach this point, all the triumph and tragedy faced on the way. They had no idea what this day meant to me, that it would secure a very personal relationship with Mickey Mantle.

Minutes ticked by agonizingly slow with no sign of a new driver. Traffic began flowing smoothly, and while it was a good sign, we had no driver. My father tried picking up my spirits, but he was angry with the driver and seemed resigned to the fact that we'd be late, likely to miss the first few innings of the real game. I wondered if I was being punished by the Gods of baseball for even thinking about losing to Elmira. I was full of guilt again, troubled and feeling alone and desperate. I began believing I'd never see Mickey Mantle, and furthermore, this was my punishment for everything I'd done against baseball.

But fate stepped in again. A new bus driver climbed aboard the bus, confident and experienced. He looked at us through the rear-view mirror and announced in a thick, New York accent, "Let's get you to the game on time."

I perked up like a dog waiting for a treat. The driver pulled out into traffic as if he'd owned the road. He navigated like a racecar driver at Daytona, passing right and left, almost as if his life depended on getting us to the ballpark on time. My mindset changed. He was making up time, but there was still a ways to go. He turned onto a busy street and for the first time we could see the outline of Yankee Stadium ahead. But only 15 minutes remained before the first pitch of the two-inning Old-Timers' game. Traffic came to a dead stop again. I began breathing as hard as I had when opening my Fort

Apache box on Christmas morning. When traffic picked up again, the driver navigated the Greyhound bus as if he'd been driving a cab. He was impressive to watch, the exact opposite of our first driver. I had sensed that he wasn't really a bus driver at all, rather an angel sent from heaven. As I thought more about it, I didn't recall how he had entered the bus. I hadn't noticed a car or another bus drop him off, only his sudden appearance. I perked up again. We passed a few more cars, then turned into a spot reserved for buses at the Yankee Stadium entrance. He pulled into an open spot, placed the bus in park and announced, "Yankee Stadium. All Depart."

As we rushed out of the bus, the driver caught my eye and winked at me knowingly. I didn't know what to say, so I said nothing. I wished later on that I had thanked him for getting us to the game on time, but I didn't. I was too wrapped-up in getting off the bus and into the stadium. We rushed like a herd towards the turnstiles, and as we did, the familiar voice of Bob Sheppard cut through the Yankee Stadium air, announcing, "Now batting… number seven… Mickey… Mantle…

We handed our tickets to the usher and rushed for our seats on the Mezzanine Level. We ran as fast as we could, dodging hundreds of fans just as our angel bus driver had done with the New York traffic. I could hear the crowd roar as Mickey took his place in the box, but obstacles were aplenty. Finally reaching the Mezzanine, I looked out onto the magnificent field of green. I could smell the freshly mowed grass, the hot dogs, cotton candy and the peanuts—no different than Johnson Field back home.

It was then I'd realized Mickey wasn't batting. Another old Yankee was. I missed him by just a few seconds. I asked my father if there was a chance he'd bat again, but the game was just two innings. We found our seats and watched the rest of the game, and he was right. Mickey's earlier at bat was the only one he'd have.

Understanding my disappointment was impossible to fathom. Even receiving a free vinyl record of Mickey's retirement ceremony from two months earlier didn't take the pain away. *A Day To Remember* record was no more than a piece of vinyl, not flesh and blood. Much as I played that record until nearly wearing out its grooves, all that happened and the way it happened was beyond unfair. Everything leading up to this moment had been stolen from me.

I waited for Mickey to come out of the dugout after the game ended, but he didn't. Even a glimpse of him would have been something. Even as the dugout emptied and a few Old-Timers' came onto the field, I didn't see Mickey.

We watched the real game between Oakland and the Yankees, a 2-1 win for the A's. But I was distracted for most of the game. My imagination took over to save me from the grips of reality. I imagined Mickey Mantle standing inside the box. He was alone on the field—not another player but him. I could see all of it just then. Home runs. Great catches. Game-winning hits. It was a moment frozen in time—my moment alone with Mickey Mantle, one I'd always envisioned and waited for all my life. As I watched him standing in that batters box, my imagination took me back to the place I had longed to be, a place where nine year old boys lived out their own dreams of being the best there was, the best there would ever be. I pulled myself back into my nine-year-old self, to a time when all was right in the world, when the Yankees were winning the World Series and Mickey Mantle was vibrant and young. It made me feel complete, as if my baseball journey with Mickey Mantle ended and a new chapter was about to begin.

Then reality pulled me back.

There was a part of me that never wanted to grow up, or to grow old or to even retire from baseball. There was a part of me that wanted to keep things just as they were. I wanted Mickey Mantle to play baseball forever, but I knew it was over. He wasn't coming back.

The bus ride home was long and tiring. Yankee Stadium was beautiful, no question about it. But the void in my life and the empty pit in my stomach was what I'd felt most. I missed seeing Mickey Mantle.

13

Redemption: Mickey's Final Homer: August 11, 1973

I reached 17 in November of 1972, and baseball still played a big part in my life. I'd finished a successful three years playing Babe Ruth ball, selected an all-star each season. Any success at the Babe Ruth level didn't seem to help or carry over into high school, cut abruptly from both varsity and junior varsity squads. The harsh reality of being cut served as another example and reminder that past successes had no bearing on future outcomes. I was stunned at first, surprised that coaches hadn't followed my career path dominating Little League and Babe Ruth for five years. Despite years of thriving and improving, I was told I wasn't good enough. Hearing those words felt no different than not making the Little League team the day Batman won over baseball. It was devastating and humiliating.

It was a wonder that anyone made either team. The lone exhibition tryout game played on the frigid-cold field of Vestal Junior High School served as my Waterloo. Early spring weather in upstate New York was not kind or appropriate for baseball—and with no protection from winter-like elements played on an open field, proper circulation to the hands was nearly impossible. So cold was the temperature and so brisk the winds that I couldn't wait for the game to end and to find some shelter and warmth. There were no dugouts to offer any relief from the cold, no coats to wear between innings. I couldn't hit the ball under such conditions—and I didn't. A foul ball that made my hands tingle and throb left me helpless at the plate. As if I'd been stung by an entire nest of bees, I felt defenseless against any pitch. Although I'd tried to muster up enough effort to swing the bat properly, I couldn't. I struck out all three times that day.

With a year off from baseball for the first time, the world and all it offered opened itself. I shed excess weight that I'd carried until I was 15, my body going through normal changes. I became more athletic and could run as fast or faster than anyone else. Then came a girlfriend, driver's license and a job after school. And as a year without baseball ended, rekindled was the desire to tryout for the varsity again.

I made the team that senior year of high school—made it as its starting second baseman. As that season progressed and my love for baseball returned, very few thoughts of Mickey Mantle entered my mind. He'd been out of baseball for four years, and the new Yankees led by Bobby Murcer had my attention. Murcer was supposed to be the next Mickey Mantle, handed that baton when Mickey retired. And while Murcer was very good, he never produced Mantle-like numbers. Hardly anyone did. Despite my love for Mickey Mantle, the hype and promotion placed on Bobby Murcer brought back my interest in the Yankees. And as Murcer became the new face of the Yankees, he became my Mickey.

Bobby Murcer didn't lead the Yankees to the AL pennant in 1972, but he did club 33 homers—nearly a third of the Yanks' 103 total. He was their dominant player, receiving little help when it came to power and knocking in runs. Had Murcer played with Mickey and Roger and the rest of my Yankees, well, who knows what he would have done. That the Yankees so depended on him at all times was truly unfair—especially the continued comparisons to Mickey. Although Bobby Murcer didn't hit 50 homers or hit a ball 500 feet or more, in my mind he was the new Mickey Mantle, and I was grateful that someone was.

Late in the baseball season, I got the chance to return to Yankee Stadium, another bus trip on Old-Timers' day. The second I was asked, memories from the first trip roared back in just seconds. Stinging memories I hadn't thought much of since that day. It certainly didn't take me long to decide what to do. I jumped at the chance.

. . . . .

I hadn't been back to the stadium since the first bus trip in 1969. Even though that day ended in bitter disappointment, I wanted to go back. I had grown out of the childlike notion of being Mickey Mantle, but wanted always to see him in person playing baseball. Gone were all the baseball fantasies and the pretending to be, but they'd been replaced by the empty pit in my stomach and memory of missing him bat by mere seconds. And now that Mickey was a scheduled player for another Old-Timers' game, thoughts of actually seeing him bat became possible and likely to happen. I'd reasoned that any chance we'd be late for the start of the game would be slim, and the bus would get to the stadium in plenty of time.

Smooth sailing at first kept me calm, and we were way ahead of schedule. But the second we hit the fringe of New York traffic, we slowed to a crawl. I looked at the driver to see if he was nervous, but he looked normal to me- as if he'd been through this before. And as we inched our way towards our destination, I started looking at the time.

Not again, I thought. I'd remembered this very route from four years ago and how long it had taken to reach the stadium. As my mind drifted back, I had a feeling that history would repeat itself. We'd be late again. I shook my head and laughed. Not a happy laugh, but a, *here we go again* laugh. I sat back and resigned myself to an inevitable outcome.

But I was 17, not 13. It wasn't bothering me as much as it had in the past, yet still was annoying and nerve-racking. It gave me time to think about things, to put everything into perspective and to remember my days as Mickey Mantle. My mind went through all of it from start to finish, every bit of it, from the Binghamton Farm League until now. As the pace of the bus picked up and our chances of being on time seemed remote at best, the old memories just wouldn't let go. It didn't matter how I'd grown out of it. It didn't matter that I'd be bound for college in less than a year. What mattered *really was* getting to the stadium in time to see Mickey Mantle bat. That's all I'd asked of the Gods of baseball. *Just get us there on time.*

I felt a renewed sense of urgency. I kept looking at the time, the traffic and the driver. I wanted badly for him to cut around the traffic, but there was nowhere to go. And just like our first trip when the traffic pattern opened up briefly, it did again. He changed lanes and moved in and out as if the other cars allowed it to happen. He dodged aggressive drivers and ignored the constant horn blowing and nasty hand gestures from others. He seemed to be on a mission exactly as our replacement driver from four years ago. There was at least a chance to make it on time as he pulled into the stadium parking lot and zoomed around other buses. He pulled into the very drop-off point from four years ago, then announced, "Yankee Stadium. All depart."

As we pushed forward and cleared the bus, we rushed for the turnstiles. With ticket in hand, I recalled the words spoken from our bus driver were the exact words spoken from our replacement driver four years ago. I turned back to get a look at him, but he remained inside the bus, the window glare blocking the view. *Weird*. I handed my ticket to the attendant and raced for the mezzanine.

Being older and faster gave me an edge I hadn't had four years ago. I zigzagged and cut around people in front of me, but the Old-Timers' game had started, the familiar voice of Bob Sheppard echoing throughout the stadium. But when he announced, "Now batting, number 7, Mickey… Mantle… I raced as fast as I could to reach any point to see the field when a sudden roar from the crowd shook the stadium like an earthquake had hit it. The deafening sound must have resulted from a Mantle home run, and as that sinking feeling of missing it expanded the empty feeling inside, a quick follow-up groan from the crowd said otherwise. "Foul Ball" we'd heard someone yell nearby, his ear glued to a transistor radio. I kept running, hoping and praying that Mickey would still be batting when I'd reach the mezzanine. I wanted him to step out of the box and look around, to give me just enough time to see him bat. It didn't matter if he'd struck out, walked or hit a home run. I was feeling like Mickey Mantle again, alive and hopeful. And as my legs churned and my prayer released, I reached the mezzanine.

As I reached the very spot I'd first laid eyes on that magnificent field of green, Mickey stood outside the box, looking around. And he did look around for a few seconds before stepping back into the box, as if he'd been waiting for some reason. I took it as a sign, as if something larger was at work and my message had made it and was answered. That momentary pause was meaningful. It wasn't for any of the other 50,000 fans in the stadium—it was for me. I believed it then and I believe it still. *Mickey Mantle had waited for me.*

Whitey delivered the next pitch, a slow-moving one, fast and over the plate. With a swing that had come from the Gods, the ball sailed high and far, rising and staying in the air as if in slow-motion. It hit its peak and descended from the sky. With head down as he took the bases, Mickey Mantle had done it again.

Hundreds of outstretched hands rose like baby birds about to be fed. Mickey circled the bases with the same hobble and limp I had come to know and copied perfectly. The crowd was in an absolute frenzy as he went around the bases slow and sure. And as Mickey touched home plate, the deafening noise continued. But I didn't hear any of it.

With tears in my eyes, I realized that my baseball life as Mickey Mantle had come full-circle—and so had his. We had been together for a long time, but only now for the first time. It had been an exceedingly long road, but all of the obstacles I'd endured made it so well worth it. And as I stood and cheered with the rest of the crowd, I watched Mickey limp towards the dugout.

I wanted to be alone with Mickey Mantle just then. I wanted to cheer him on and for him to notice me standing in the walkway of the mezzanine section. I wanted him to look up at me and tip his cap—just enough to know it was for me. I wanted Mickey Mantle to acknowledge our relationship—just this once. And I felt grateful for all of it. Grateful that somehow—*somehow*—in this truly unbelievable ending to our relationship, we'd made it home together.

It was Mickey Mantle's final home run.

14

Final Thoughts: Cooperstown, N.Y. National Baseball Hall of Fame, July 6, 2016 "A Day Unlike All Others."

"The world is so unpredictable. Things happen suddenly, unexpectedly. We want to feel we are in control of our own existence. In some ways we are, in some ways we're not. We are ruled by the forces of chance and coincidence."

~Paul Auster

I've been a firm believer in meaningful synchronicity and Divine Intervention for quite some time. Personal experience has taught me that. Not just a few experiences over the course of these 60+ years, but many. I've learned to read signs life has planted and recognize events aligning in uncanny and unbelievable ways. It is awe-inspiring, humbling and profoundly spiritual.

"Coincidence," points out author V.C. King is "The probability of a certain set of circumstances coming together in a meaningful (or tragic) way is so low that it simply cannot be considered mere coincidence."

You run into an old friend in the most unlikely of places, purely by chance. A few seconds separation and it doesn't happen. To call that a coincidence is natural, I suppose. But chance meetings like this happen all the time to all of us. Sometimes they take decades—weaving slowly towards the finish line. To the untrained mind, coincidence prevails. But why or how do such things happen so frequently? Multifaceted events linked in perfect order that seem to have a plan and purpose. Author J.M. Darhower puts it beautifully, stating, "*Yes, you see, there's no such thing as coincidence. There are no accidents in life. Everything that happens is the result of a calculated move that leads us to where we are.*"

The saying, "It's a small world," is for good reason. This gigantic world occupied by billions of people, full of astonishing coincidences that are hard to believe and harder yet to comprehend. I'll venture to say this phrase is repeated dozens of times a year, and that's by each and every one of use. And for those buying into the concept that "good" coincidence is dependent upon "Divine Intervention," then you'll follow the course of this introduction with nods of approval. For others with no belief or borderline belief, well, read on. While I have no ulterior motive in converting non- believers, what happened to me in Cooperstown defies logic, at the very least.

When my father-in-law John Gillard died just over 20 years ago, my wife and I (along with our two young daughters) stayed at her childhood home for the funeral. In the wee hours of the morning of the funeral, she awoke suddenly and went out to the living room. She'd "Felt compelled," she'd told me later, deciding for no reason at all to look out the living room window and onto the street where our car was parked in front of the house. And at that very moment, a local furniture store truck drove by and clipped the rear-view mirror of our car. The driver didn't stop or slow down. I'm sure he had no idea he was being watched by my wife, so on he drove.

But she recognized the furniture store's name painted on the side of the truck. A few hours later when the store opened, she called to report what happened. While we can only guess what happened to the driver of that truck, the store's owner took responsibility and paid for the damages.

We talked about that incident as if it truly were a "Divine Intervention." We mentioned the story at the eulogy. We spoke about it at length and could hardly believe what it took for this "coincidence" to occur and how it played out in such precise measure. We recognized that something beyond our understanding was able to lead my wife to that window at that exact moment in time. Her father had sent us a sign.

While coincidence disguises itself often as something else, what of fate and destiny? That divine inspired (controlled) predetermined script that is our life. We're on this stage performing, acting out our lines, only we don't know the script. And while we are busy writing one out every waking minute of the day (thanks to the freedom of free will and decision-making), the die has been cast. The script has been set in stone. States author David Richo; *"We do not create our own destiny; we participate in its unfolding. Synchronicity works as a catalyst toward the working out of that destiny."*

And as we're busy playing out our roles and playing the part with our free will, we really don't see that far ahead. In fact, whether we've rehearsed what we'd prefer in our lives and played it out in our minds a million times, we really don't see what's coming. We may be proactive and organized and thoughtful, doing what we can in aligning future events towards a comforting and predictable outcome. But we really don't know. And while predictability can be comforting or distressing, it is the outcome that often leaves us bemused and even humbled.

This little stand I've taken for coincidence and fate is a mere prelude for an extremely personal and spiritual experience in July of 2016. And while this orchestrated story ends so beautifully in Cooperstown, N.Y., its roots stretch clear back some 50 years ago to when it started. And as I've had time to reflect on what it has taken for the whole thing to materialize, I remain awestruck, captivated from what has happened to me, and at what lengths fate will go to make it so. Mesmerized, even as a true believer in such things.

So on we travel to Cooperstown, home to the National Baseball Hall of Fame and Museum, where every element of Divine Intervention, fate, and synchronicity was at work in the making of this story.

It begins in the middle of the 1960's, our first (and only) family trip to Cooperstown. While my memory is distinct and so very clear on most episodes from my childhood, I have little recollection of our visit to the Hall of Fame. Perhaps I was just a bit too young to grasp what the Baseball Hall of Fame stood for, or that a museum was just too big and likely bored me. I simply don't remember. And while my father filmed parts of that day on an old 35mm camera, the grainy film has triggered no memories from the corners of my mind. It is particularly surprising my memory has failed me here. Baseball began its grip on me right around that time period. And while I'm sure our tour was utter and complete, nothing we'd experienced that day resonates with me at all.

Despite the fact we had grown up with baseball in our blood and developed a great love for our New York Yankees, that day trip to

Cooperstown would be our last. A 90 minute drive so within our reach. And as the years have passed and the distance to Cooperstown has lengthened due to family commitments and relocations, any thoughts of returning rarely crossed my mind. Content I was to enjoy baseball for what it was. Content to leave Cooperstown alone, to allow its history to grow and strengthen without any sense of curiosity within me. And as much as I love the game, its history and nostalgia, thoughts of Cooperstown were being suppressed for some reason.

Fifty years later, the stories of my life in the 60's began their avalanche upon me. Dreams and memories, so pure and unbroken were being made clear to me. When I'd decided to write this book, I whizzed through the writing process in short order, amazed at not only what I'd written, but to all I'd recalled. And as one chapter rolled into another, I was on target to finish in just a few months. Then in April of 2015, I stopped writing.

No matter how hard I tried, nothing was coming to me. I'd hit the wall of writing and couldn't understand why. The book needed a proper ending, and while the final home run hit by Mickey in the Old-Timers' game certainly had the makings for one, there was something still missing. There was a void to the story, something significant. As I tried to find the right words for what I hoped would be a fitting conclusion, nothing I wrote or remembered seemed to fit. There was no spark to the words. Nothing seemed appropriate. I put it down for a few days and hoped the right story would come to me. But nothing did. The great memories that flowed like a river at the beginning dried up. The corners of my mind displaying baseball memories had emptied. The manuscript sat on my desk for 15 months.

Then in July of 2016, I was invited by Cooperstown Crier newspaper Editor Greg Klein to cover and write a story at the National Baseball Hall of Fame. Nancy Churnin- a fellow-member of, *The Hoy For the Hall Committee,* had written a children's baseball book set to be interviewed at the Hall. Klein knew I was familiar with the topic and had a writing background. I accepted his invitation enthusiastically. Unexpectedly, the rules of chance and coincidence merged in a very big way. That day and its events turned out to be the missing link to finishing my story.

To say I was looking forward to that day is a giant understatement. As one of 11 members of, *The Hoy For The Hall Committee,* finally I'd meet three of our members, including Churnin and two Deaf members, Steve Sandy and Peter Rozynski. I'd get to write an article at the Baseball Hall of Fame- an honor I'd never conceived or thought of- and have an opportunity to tour the museum, something I hadn't done in over 50 years.

I stayed at a quaint, little motel about a mile from the Hall of Fame and ventured into town quite early the day of Churnin's interview. With several hours to kill, I wanted to explore as much as I could, to take it all in, to bring back some old baseball memories from more than 50 years ago. I began my tour by walking down Main Street toward the Hall and noticed a sign indicating, *Doubleday Field*. For some reason, I imagined Doubleday Field being on the outskirts of town, surrounded by a parking lot. But it wasn't. It was right in front of me.

I walked toward the stadium and stood alone in the parking lot, admiring the structure. I took several pictures and walked a bit closer, eager to examine any plaques or inscriptions. As I drew nearer I was surprised that the entrance to the stadium was open. I walked the ramp up toward the grandstand, checking out old photos of old players and memories along the wall. And that's when I lost it emotionally.

I began to weep uncontrollably as old memories of 1965 overcame me suddenly. It was the year the Yankees were scheduled to play the Phillies in the annual Hall of Fame game. It was the year I'd asked my father repeatedly if we could go to that game, to see the Yankees play, to see Mickey Mantle.

But life got in the way. I'm sure tickets were extremely difficult to come by. We didn't know anyone with tickets. Or perhaps the game had been sold-out long before I'd started to badger my father. For whatever reason, it wasn't his fault. We didn't make that baseball pilgrimage to Doubleday Field, and I didn't get to see Mickey up close and personal. I was devastated beyond words.

But I'd suppressed those memories until that very moment, standing alone in the shadows of the grandstand, crying as if I were that 9-year-old boy just being told by his father that we would not be going to the game. With tears streaming down my face, I took a right and walked slowly up the last aisle of the grandstand and sat down near the top row of the old, gray bleachers. I was drunk with emotion and looked onto the field and around the stadium. I began imagining my Yankees on that field just then: Joe

Pepitone, Clete Boyer, Roger Maris and Mickey Mantle. As I placed them one by one into their positions across the diamond, I swear I could see Mickey in the outfield looking at me and tipping his cap.

The tears continued. I began texting my wife and two daughters of what I was experiencing. Imagination or not, the feeling of stepping back in time was surreal, and I didn't want it to end. I was totally alone and immersed with my Yankees. I walked over to the bleachers near first base for a closer look at the field hoping the entrance to the field was open. But it wasn't. I wanted badly to walk the outfield grass where Mickey once stood. I wanted to experience how it felt to be near him as the 9-year-old boy I had become again, walking the same path my hero once had. I sat there for several hours, all alone in the grandstand watching *my field of dreams*. A peace I'd never felt before settled over me. I was completely alone and sharing *my memories with my old team*. I took more pictures. I talked to the invisible players. It was time to leave.

Methodically I walked the ramp down. I scanned every inch of the stadium and field, storing every image from the dugouts to the outfield walls. And as I stepped outside the stadium and into the parking lot, cars began filtering in- at first just one or two, but within five minutes, a dozen or more. Young boys dressed in baseball uniforms emerged from the cars, yawning and stretching. Several coaches began gathering the boys together onto both sides of the field. I walked over and asked someone if there was a game being played. And there was, with two 13-year-old teams scheduled to play in less than an hour. The chance to walk the outfield was still alive.

• • • • •

I approached two coaches of the Anjo Bombers, assistants Richard Whipple and Roger Furmanski. I introduced myself and immediately began recounting what had happened. With both men reacting favorably, I asked for a few minutes in the outfield, how vital it was for me to walk in Mickey's footsteps. The pair seemed to recognize my pure emotions, I was certain of that. They'd bought-into my story for sure. Whipple said, "Lets go out there together. I'll take some pictures of you wherever you'd like to stand."

Together we walked the outfield, taking it slow and easy. Whipple began commenting about my purpose right then, giving the impression that he understood completely my feelings. He seemed to be enjoying that moment with me, caring enough to not only guide me around the field, but to relate and comment with some of his own baseball memories. We had met just minutes earlier, and struck a bond – baseball bringing us together like old friends. Even as strangers, the infinite language of baseball had brought us together as part of the design- part of the final equation to my story. It was as simple as that for me.

We reached deep outfield and Richard took some photos of me. I walked out near the warning track, believing I was standing exactly where Mickey Mantle once stood. Richard snapped several more pictures of me and I envisioned Mickey standing next to me. I walked around the outfield and the warning track, full of peace and wonder and grateful for what was happening. I looked in towards home plate and it seemed to be a mile away. A new respect for what it would take to hit a ball over these fences came to mind. The spaciousness of the field and the ground an outfielder needed to cover just to catch a fly ball was never more evident. While I'd played organized baseball on regulation-sized fields in my youth, recalling any feelings of being swallowed-up by their dimensions went missing. Perhaps the grandstand and bleachers played tricks on my mind, for never had I played in a stadium seating thousands. Admiration and a newfound appreciation for all baseball players came to mind. As we began our walk back in from the outfield, we spoke more of baseball history, the Yankees and Mickey Mantle. I thanked Richard for what he'd done for me, and several coaches tipped their caps. I returned to the bleachers to watch a few innings of the game, then headed for town to explore some more.

Several hours later, Nancy Churnin took center stage at the Bullpen Theater. I was proud as could be as she cruised through the interview. She answered the questions like a champion. She seemed entirely natural in her position on stage, and I wanted badly to capture the essence of her interview with my story. I took notes and stayed around for several hours as she signed books. When she'd finished, I headed for the Hall's library.

I had done some soul-searching for several hours following the incident on Doubleday Field, doubting that any of this was spiritual in nature. Perhaps my imagination was playing tricks on me, and my emotions were running high from the surroundings and circumstances. And I wondered if Mickey had even played, if he'd even made the trip, for injuries had often left him off the field. I had to know the truth.

I asked the librarian if she would print the story from that game in 1965 and provide me with its box score. She located the game account in just seconds and printed it promptly. Scanning the story, I looked for Mickey's name- it wasn't mentioned. Slowing down my pace, I looked again and it wasn't there. No mention of his name at all. Doubts and fears filled my mind again.

· · · · ·

Certainly the odds of Mickey playing in that game decidedly went down. That his name wasn't mentioned in the story seemed unusual. The Yanks scored seven runs and won the game. Had Mickey played in that game, in all likelihood he would have participated in its scoring. I asked her again if there was a box score to the game. There was not. I pushed her for more, but there was nothing to be found. I was terribly disappointed but wasn't about to give up. Feeling somewhat defeated, I began an Internet search for the box score, but found nothing. One link led to the other, but the search started going off course. The ever-important box score was missing.

The thought came to try goggling, *scorecard* or *program*. Scrolling and looking through each listing, a sepia scorecard from *that very game* finally popped up. It was for sale. Pausing and closing my eyes, I wished for Mickey's name to be in that box score. With one eye open, I keyed it in and clicked on the scorecard and noticed lineups from both teams running down its side like any other scorecard. I clicked on the Yankees lineup and followed it down.

And there it was—batting third and playing left field- *Mickey Mantle*.

It didn't matter that his only hit was a double and hadn't contributed much in the 7-4 victory over the Phillies. Verification was what I was after. Discovering Mickey's name on the lineup card validated any strong connections I'd felt. Elation and euphoria set in.

Hours after touring the Hall, I stepped outside to put the whole day together in my mind. What a day it had been—one of the best ever. Slowly I walked up and down Main Street one last time before heading home, pausing at each store, admiring storefront windows displaying baseball uniforms, photos and autographed baseballs. That's when the urge to buy something made me stop for a moment.

. . . . .

It didn't feel right that I'd leave without some souvenir to remember the trip by. Perhaps a Mickey Mantle autographed baseball or a photo of him, or an old Yankees yearbook or Mantle jersey. And as I looked up and down the street and contemplated these choices, I decided on a Mickey Mantle baseball card.

Treasured like no other baseball card, Mickey Mantle's card was the most sought after of all during my youth. As the decades rolled by, those treasures had been discarded or thrown away. And for that I was angry with myself. Value aside, nostalgia was more important now. Vividly I'd recalled each card and pose that Mickey and all other players from those years had been in for their baseball card. More flashbacks as I walked across the street to *Yaz Sports*.

Turning the corner before entering the store I'd noticed some paper money lying on a patch of grass nearby. Dozens of people passed, but not a soul noticed the money. Nobody was checking their pockets or wearing a panicked expression that comes when realizing money was lost. Collectively they'd kept walking past me, going about their business. So I reached down and picked up the money. One dollar. Chuckling, I placed the bill into my pocket when a voice nearby said, "Thank you." The man was seated nearby, and I asked him if the money was his. Instead, he said he was a local resident and thought I'd been picking trash up from the ground. I nodded and told him it was only a dollar bill, understanding the importance he'd placed on keeping the grounds of Main Street impeccably clean. The dollar bill seemed to be the only paper on the ground as far as the eye could see. So odd it seemed that not another soul noticed it. I thought back to how a single dollar would have been enough for 20 packs of baseball cards. *Great times*, I'd thought. I opened the door to *Yaz Sports* and went inside.

It took just a few seconds to find the baseball cards. Row after row in open glass displays filled the place, players listed alphabetically. I found the Mickey Mantle row in a few seconds, then finger-walked it, pausing at each card and remembering that I'd owned every one. I turned cards over to check stats and comments, stopping at the 1969 card, its short comment of card #500 reading, *The All-Star announced his retirement from baseball on March 1st, 1969. This is the one,* I'd thought.

I'd noticed the entire collection of cards as imitations, authentic cards protected behind glass. But it didn't matter. The image of Mickey swinging the bat on any baseball card- authentic or imitation- was good enough. Then the irony hit me—and I realized why an imitation card was appropriate. For when I was nine, I was nothing more than an imitation of Mickey Mantle, pretending to be him. Certainly it seemed the right and only thing to do. I took the card to the cashier.

"That'll be one dollar," he said.

"Just a dollar?" I asked.

"Just a dollar."

Reaching into my pocket I held the crisp dollar bill found outside moments ago. I smiled knowingly just then, shaking my head at how random it seemed. But it wasn't random at all. It had been planned. And so I paid him with that dollar bill I'd found on the ground outside his store. No sales tax was charged. It was exactly one dollar.

Arrangements like this one are hard to believe. But I was absolutely sure it had been Mickey Mantle planting that dollar just for me. Dozens of people passed by that bill before I had noticed it, but on they went about their business. As I drew a mental line to the synchronicity of that moment and the entire day, I was sure it was Mickey's way of acknowledging that 9-year-old boy whose heart had been broken by not being at that game in 1965. It was Mickey's way of thanking me for playing my part, for following his career and for pretending to be him for so long. It was his way of saying, "This one's on me, kid."

I told my wife and two daughters about my experience that day, but not to another soul. I wrote everything down while it was still fresh in my mind, wanting and needing to have a permanent written reminder as to exactly what occurred that day. And after several weeks of soul-searching, I decided to send the story into the Crier to see if they'd be interested in running it. A few weeks passed and no response. Of course they had likely read it and scoffed at the preposterous nature of the story. Maybe it was too edgy to run, too spiritual to share with such a large audience. But editor Greg Klein instead asked me to send it again, that he hadn't received it in his emails. And so I did.

That same day he emailed back, stating, "This is great stuff." Several days later, I received an email from editor Sam Pollak of The Oneonta Sun. Pollack wrote, "This is one of the best reads of the year." He called me and we discussed what happened that day. The story ran on page one of the August 25, 2017 Edition of, *The Cooperstown Crier*.

I don't think I can capture that magical day any better with words. A final tribute to Mickey Mantle and my visit to Cooperstown was the final puzzle piece for the ending to this book and what I had been searching for. This entire story seemingly ruled entirely by the forces of chance and coincidence right from the start. I am certain that my visit to Cooperstown was meant to be. The process to completing its course and unfolding itself in such a way has humbled me entirely. It has overwhelmed me. An unbelievable feeling of fulfillment and awakening runs through my veins and will forever. It was entirely worth waiting for.

Once upon a time at the age of nine, I clubbed more home runs than any player in the history of baseball. I had believed I was the greatest player in the history of the game, and no future player would ever come close to matching my home runs totals.

Turns out I was wrong.

Of course I'd heard of Babe Ruth, everyone had. I understood he'd hit a zillion homers, maybe more. And while he played about a thousand years earlier, I couldn't conceive that Ruth- or any other player for that matter- accumulated more home runs than Mickey Mantle. It just couldn't be. Mickey Mantle was the all-time home run leader.

But as my childhood gave way to the teens, discoveries were made and the truth was revealed. Although I could see in black and white that Babe Ruth was indeed the home run champion of all time, still I'd felt happy that Mickey was third all-time at his retirement in 1969. I wasn't upset that in the very near future others would pass him by, and by 1972 had dropped to 5th, plummeting to 18th by 2017. It gave me reason to examine my home run totals from years playing organized baseball- discounting, of course, the unknown numbers accumulated playing in the Binghamton Farm League. It didn't take long to do the math. I had never even hit one.

The irony that I came within inches of hitting a homer in my first at bat as a 10 year old Little Leaguer wasn't lost on me. From the moment I'd launched that rocket off of my bat and came so close to feeling the elation of hitting a homer over the fence, I knew inside there would be many more opportunities to hit a ton of them. Undoubtedly I'd lead the league in homers for every season on every team I'd play for. But it didn't happen in the Little League, Babe Ruth League or high school.

For those few years in the mid 1960's when I pretended to be Mickey Mantle, well, they will live in me until my final breath is taken. Forever I'll be grateful to my favorite hero of them all, grateful for what he did to help shape my life and for being at my side during those early years, and even for the dormant ones later on. I feel a special privilege and unique connection and bonding to Mickey Mantle that had been inside me for 50 years. And while I'd never experienced the feeling of hitting a baseball over the fence, nothing could replace the feeling of being Mickey Mantle—even for just a while.

About the Author

Gary Kaschak has served as stringer, sports writer and/or columnist for The *Vestal News* (upper New York State), The *Green Bay Press Gazette* (Wisconsin) and the *Burlington County Times* (New Jersey). He served the *Montrose Independent* (Pennsylvania) as its Sports Editor. He was for some time a game-day Statistician of the Washington Federals (a team in the now-defunct United States Football League {USFL}; and he's served as sports reporter for WKOP radio, out of Binghamton, New York.

My Name Was Mickey Mantle is his fourth novel. He has also authored *Hands That Break... Hands That Heal, The Hole To China,* and *Lifestone.* He lives with his wife, Maureen, in Cedarbrook, New Jersey.

For more information please visit:
www.garydkaschak.com

View other Black Rose Writing titles at www.blackrosewriting.com/books and use promo code **PRINT** to receive a **20% discount** when purchasing.

www.ingramcontent.com/pod-product-compliance
Lightning Source LLC
Chambersburg PA
CBHW052210090526
44584CB00016BA/2035